On Higher Ground

Education and the Case for Affirmative Action

On Higher Ground

Education and the Case for Affirmative Action

WALTER FEINBERG

Foreword by JULIAN BOND

Teachers College, Columbia University
New York and London

Published by Teachers College Press, 1234 Amsterdam Avenue, New York, NY 10027

Library of Congress Cataloging-in-Publication Data

Feinberg, Walter, 1937–
    On higher ground : education and the case for affirmative action /
Walter Feinberg ; foreword by Julian Bond.
      p.   cm.
    Includes bibliographical references (p.   ) and index.
    ISBN 0-8077-3699-6 (cloth). – ISBN 0-8077-3698-8 (pbk.)
    1. Discrimination in education – United States – Prevention.
2. Affirmative action programs – United States.   3. Educational
equalization – United States.   4. Minorities – Education – United
States.   I. Title.
LC212.2.F45   1997
379.2′6′0973 – dc21   97-26160

ISBN 0-8077-3698-8 (paper)
ISBN 0-8077-3699-6 (cloth)

Printed on acid-free paper
Manufactured in the United States of America

05   04   03   02   01   00   99   98   8 7 6 5 4 3 2 1

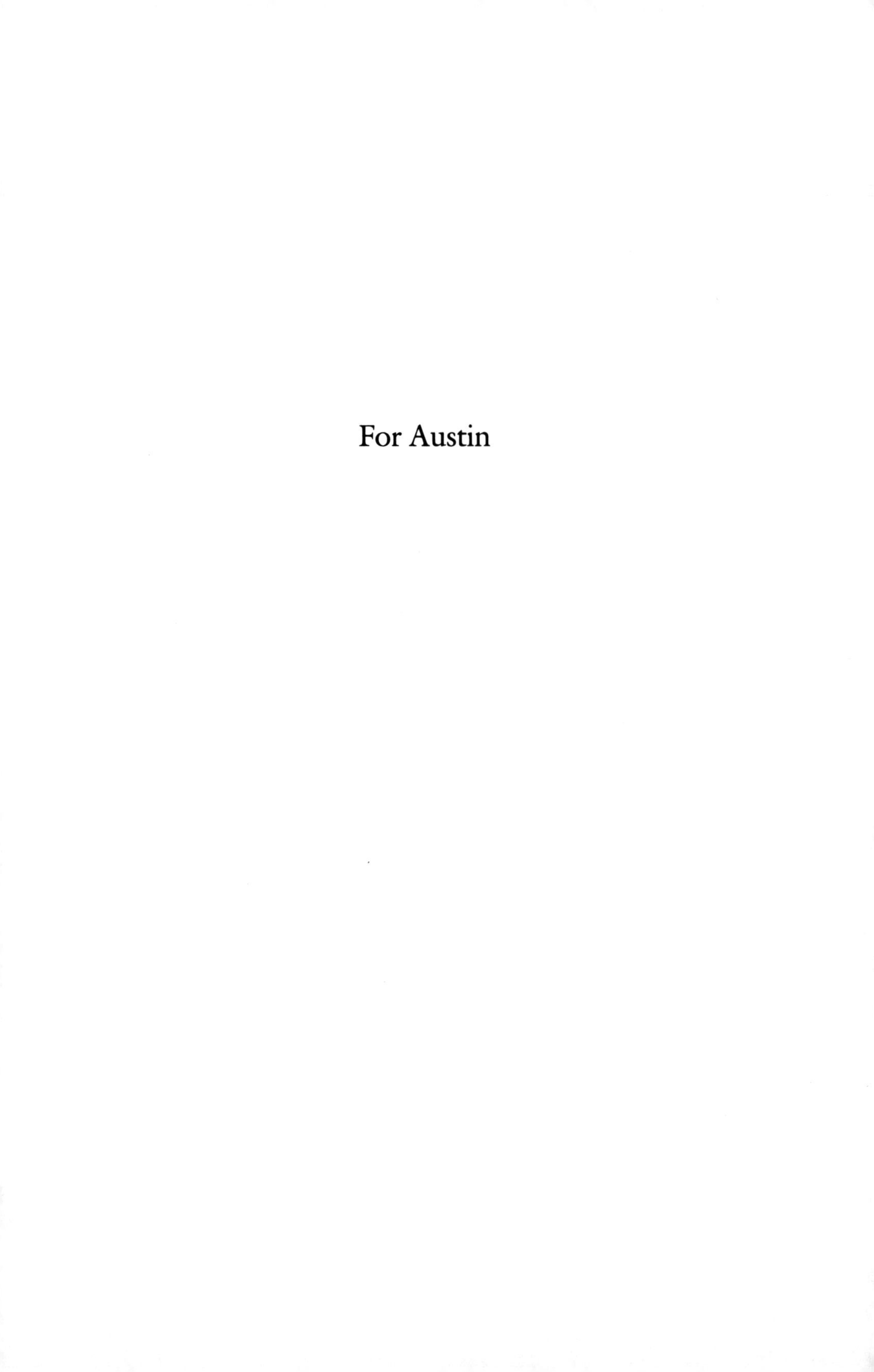

For Austin

Contents

Foreword

Two words—affirmative action—are among the most contentious in American public life. In the 1996 Presidential contest, all of the Republican candidates for president made trashing affirmative action a centerpiece of their campaigns. The winner, President Bill Clinton, promised to mend rather than end affirmative action programs.

As Clinton was winning, California voters approved a measure eliminating affirmative action programs in education, and a year later, a Federal court in Texas sharply restricted the use of race in university admissions in Texas, Louisiana, and Mississippi. One result has been a decrease in Black applications to undergraduate and professional schools at the University of California. At the University of Texas School of Law in Austin, Black admissions dropped from 65 in 1996 to five in 1997. Elsewhere there are predictions of equally dire results if current affirmation action is weakened or eliminated.

Advocates for and opponents of affirmative action remain as quarrelsome now as ever. Armed with a large catalogue of anecdotal reports of illiterate Blacks stealing jobs from White MIT graduates or 95-pound women replacing linebacker-sized White men as shipyard stevedores, opponents have created widespread dissatisfaction and unease with race- and gender-centered approaches, which seem unfair on their face; after all, don't we live in a meritocracy? Aren't the pampered children of Black millionaires taking college seats that ought to go to the hard-working offspring of White plumbers? Doesn't using race and gender as a partial basis for hiring or college admissions mean that color and sex have now become qualifications, and merit is cast aside? Doesn't affirmative action actually create low self-esteem in its beneficiaries?

On the other hand, supporters often seem unable to offer logical arguments in favor of using race to, as a Supreme Court Justice put it, get beyond race. As one might expect, the dispute has been a bonanza for many—there is a small but growing library of books extolling its benefits or explicating its harms. But Walter Feinberg has produced a volume that elevates the debate. In strong support of gender- and race-based policies, he offers a moral defense of such preferences.

Readers who favored such methods in the past but find them wanting today, or those who have always considered affirmative action equal to reverse discrimination, will find no comfort in these pages. However, those who stand strongly with using race and gender to surmount discrimination against women and minorities but have felt outgunned in today's hostile climate will discover much useful ammunition to aim at and defeat their adversaries.

White supremacy—embodied in slavery and racial prejudice—is America's original sin, and centuries of bias have flowed from it until this day. America has struggled fitfully to overcome this shameful legacy, not without some success, but no one would deny we are far from the goal of equality, more than a century after civil war ended human bondage and decades after civil rights laws made discrimination illegal. Feinberg's case is principled and ethical and represents a reasoned discussion of the costs we all pay and the benefits we all receive as we try to overcome this sorry history and dismaying present. He carefully considers—and rejects—the arguments that need-based affirmative action could ever be a satisfactory substitute for programs based on race and gender. He might have reminded us that no one beat Rodney King because he was poor.

Feinberg's reasoning will not meet every person's argument against affirmative action; it certainly will not sway determined opponents who believe we now live in a color-blind world. And it will not be read at all by those who like to quote Martin Luther King's 1963 March on Washington speech in which he spoke of the day when his children would be judged by their character and not their skin. Feinberg reminds us that King's speech was a dream, a hopeful fantasy yet unrealized. These pages detail what is required to make that dream real today.

—Julian Bond

Acknowledgments

This research was funded in part by a grant from the Spencer Foundation. Appreciation to James Anderson, David Blacker, Eric Bredo, Nick Burbules, Pradeep Dhillon, Belden Fields, Phil Jackson, Julian Bond, Deborah Merit, Ralph Page, and William Trent for their helpful comments and suggestions. My conversations with Jefferson McMahan were especially helpful in developing my ideas on the nature of the historical debt. Sections were read at the University of Chicago where I spent the 1995–1996 year as the Benton Scholar and at the University of Virginia. I am indebted to the students and faculty at these institutions and at the University of Illinois for their thoughtful comments.

I was most fortunate to have Maria Seferian as my assistant. She not only aided my search for material, but she was a most thoughtful critic whose insightful comments on earlier versions of this manuscript were very helpful.

CHAPTER 1

Toward a Theory of Affirmative Action

On July 20, 1995, the University of California Board of Regents, in response to an executive order by the governor to "end preferential treatment and to promote individual opportunity based on merit," issued a resolution that prohibited the university from using race, religion, sex, ethnicity, or national origin as a criterion for admission. A year after this resolution was issued the voters of California endorsed a similar resolution extending the ban to other institutions. California is in the vanguard of a nationwide reaction against affirmative action, but it is a reaction that is built on distortions and misunderstandings of the idea of affirmative action.

The Regents' juxtaposition of "preferential treatment" and "individual opportunity" expresses the basic assumptions behind this distortion—that there is something fundamentally inconsistent with advancing people according to their merit while addressing the historical mistreatment of groups and the stigmatization of their members, and that there is something inherently unjust in considering gender or racial or ethnic membership in advancing individuals.

Both conservatives and liberals are uneasy about affirmative action because both believe that it is primarily about economic advancement. Conservatives hold that affirmative action is primarily about a person's ability to contribute to the larger economic well-being of the nation and hold that it is a poor substitute for psychometric or market indicators of merit. Some liberal critics are uneasy about affirmative action because they think that it has failed to reduce poverty. Both of these understandings of affirmative action are inadequate and threaten to weaken the central goal of the program, which is to advance the cause of justice for people who have been stigmatized because they share certain characteristics that have been unfairly devalued by society. This book seeks to correct this misunderstanding and to develop a theory of affirmative action that will allow a more refined understanding of its uses and misuses.

1

THE POLITICAL AND ECONOMIC CLIMATE FOR THE BACKLASH AGAINST PRESENT RACE- AND GENDER-BASED POLICY

The arguments against affirmative action are not new, and most have been voiced in one way or another since the policy was formulated. However, in the last few years they have gained considerable ground as the economic stakes have risen. The continuing economic fears of the middle class, the loss of manufacturing jobs, and the downsizing of many corporations create a difficult climate for implementing affirmative action policy. The increasingly globalized economy makes many once locally rooted firms accountable to a management thousands of miles away, often residing in a different country. This distance reduces the level of local corporate responsibility and the sense of corporate citizenship.

The fact that many of the most profound causes of middle-class insecurity are beyond the control of any single person leads to a close scrutiny of more proximate factors, such as affirmative action hiring. The easy flow of capital from one area of the globe to another means that American labor often competes at a disadvantage with global capital. Many jobs that were once secure because of an advantage gained by manufacturers who located close to their main markets now disappear almost overnight because modern means of transportation and communication have diminished the advantage. Yet the effects of globalization are not easily seen or controlled. The beneficiaries of affirmative action policy make for much easier targets than do international conglomerates, creating a climate in which arguments against affirmative action are amplified, echoing off the walls created by changing global economics and resulting middle-class anxiety.

Although the arguments made against affirmative action have been amplified by present economic trends, the actual advances made by the targeted groups are quite mixed, in part due to a steady slowing of the commitment to an aggressive affirmative action stance. Despite claims to the contrary, progress for African Americans has been slowed significantly in a number of important professional fields: whereas blacks represent over 12% of the population, they comprise only 4.2% of the doctors, 3.3% of the lawyers, 5% of the university teachers, 3.7% of the engineers. The percentage of Black lawyers and judges rose from 1983 to 1993 but by only .1% and the number of Black college teachers rose by just .4% during the same period.

Moreover, salary equity continues to be an elusive goal. The average salary of White women was reported in 1995 as 70.8% of the salary of White men; for Black women the figure is 63.7% and for Hispanic women it is 53.9%. And the salaries of Black and Hispanic men relative to those of White men actually dropped from 1975 to 1993. Moreover, while a smaller percentage of White men are in the active labor force now than in 1970, there has been a larger percentage drop for Black males: from 74.3% for Black men in 1975 to 74% in 1993 and from 72.1% for Hispanic men in 1975 to 64.8% in 1993 (Roberts, 1995).

Although affirmative action has not brought the level of redistribution that the present attacks on it might lead one to believe, it has resulted in important positive change. For example, the percentage of women lawyers and judges increased from a mere 3.8% in 1972 to 22.8% in 1993, and that of women faculty members in colleges and universities rose from 28% in 1972 to 42.5% in 1993. African-American representation within some trade and blue-collar groups has increased substantially. And while the percentage of Black lawyers has remained essentially the same from 1983 to 1993, Black fire fighters, police, and other protective services in the blue- or gray-collar sections has risen by almost 4%. Similarly, the percentage of African-American cashiers has increased during the same period by more than 3% (Bureau of the Census, 1994). Thus the truth seems to be that affirmative action has made an impact in some areas for some groups but the record is spotty at best.

Progress in salary equity has also occurred in some areas. For example, the income gap between Black and White married couples narrowed from 1979 to 1993 (Stone, 1995). However, this kind of progress hardly suggests—especially given a shrinking percentage of married couples as a proportion of the general population—that affirmative action has resulted in the kind of redistribution of income, status, or well-being that would explain the latest assault on these programs. Affirmative action—while not the major source of the problem—serves as an easy target, and the present economic climate helps to stimulate the search for alternatives to race- and gender-based affirmative action and amplifies the opposing arguments considerably.

Higher education is another arena for affirmative action and enrollment of targeted groups continues to increase. The number of women has grown considerably since the advent of affirmative action programs, and in 1993 they made up over 55% of the students in higher education (Barbett et al., 1995). Minority enrollment too has risen. From 1992 to 1993 increases in enrollment occurred in all relevant categories of minorities.

The number of Hispanic and Asian Pacific Islander students increased by 3.6 percent and 3.9 percent, respectively, while the number of American Indians/Alaskan Natives and nonresident aliens increased by 2 percent. The

> number of black, non Hispanic students increased by 1.3 percent. . . . The
> number of minority students increased in 4-year institutions for all minority
> groups, ranging from a 2.5 percent increase for black students to an almost 7
> percent increase for American Indian/Alaskan Natives. (Barbett et al., 1995,
> pp. iii–iv)

Although it is a mistake to assume that all of the increase is due to affirmative action, there is little doubt that without the stimulation it provides, the enrollment picture would be significantly different. More recently, the assault on affirmative action in Texas and California has contributed to a dramatic decline in the number of applications by Blacks and Hispanics to the top state law schools.

WHAT IS AFFIRMATIVE ACTION?

Affirmative action is a set of laws, policies, guidelines, and administrative practices that is intended to end discrimination that violates the inherent equality of persons by discriminating against individuals on the grounds "that they are inferior or different" (Rosenfeld, 1991). Usually affirmative action policy aims to (1) reduce present discrimination with (2) the intent of increasing the number of targeted minorities and women in universities and colleges and at all levels of the work force.

Both sides of the definition of affirmative action are important. Much like other policies, affirmative action seeks to eliminate discrimination on the basis of race or other extraneous grounds. In this respect it is similar to laws that disallow redlining by banks or restrictive covenants by home-owner associations. These laws tell people what they may not do with regard to certain otherwise private acts. If a homeowners' association discriminates against Jews in its covenant, a nondiscrimination law requires it must stop doing so and sell to anyone–Christian, Jew, Muslim–who wants to buy a home in the area and can afford to do so. However, nondiscrimination laws do not actively seek to increase the number of previously discriminated against people in a given area. They simply aim to make acts of exclusion that are based on extraneous factors, such as race, religion, ethnicity, gender, and so forth, illegal. Once the laws are enacted, however, it is usually a matter of legal indifference whether members of the previously excluded group choose to apply. If Jews have learned they are unwelcome in an area, they may still choose to stay out of it even if they know that existing homeowners are obliged to sell to them.

Affirmative action goes beyond nondiscrimination laws because, in addition to eliminating legalized discrimination, it also actively aims to increase the number of woman and targeted minorities in certain positions. Hence some conservative critics view it in terms of legalized "discrimination," where,

> it is permissible for employees to engage in "voluntary" discrimination in favor of groups protected under the statute [the Civil Rights Act of 1964 and related laws], even though the most rigorous disparate impact tests are used to monitor discrimination against members of protected groups. (Epstein, 1995, p. 179)

The term *discrimination* has a double force in the above quotation. It rightly holds that, as a consequence of affirmative action, members of different groups are often treated differently, but it insinuates that such treatment is unfair and should be rejected.

Because affirmative action has both passive (eliminate discrimination) and active (increase the numbers of women and targeted minorities in certain positions) components, the term embraces a variety of laws, court rulings, procedures, practices, policies, and attitudes. They include a requirement that special efforts be made to go beyond traditional and entrenched networks based on gender or racial identity when seeking people to interview for positions. The idea here is that individuals of the dominant race or gender often form networks of inclusion and that when positions become available, those who are already employed will look toward people like themselves to fill them. The special effort requirement is intended to increase the pool of applicants by requiring that positions be advertised on a wide scale. This requirement not only has a favorable impact on otherwise excluded minorities and women, but it assures that White men outside of previously exclusive networks will be advised of openings.

The goal of inclusion not only influences the way in which positions are advertised; it also has an influence on the behavior permitted in the workplace by requiring employers to maintain a nonracist, nonsexist culture. If, for example, a woman mechanic's efficiency and thus her prospects for advancement are reduced as a result of a sexist environment at work, say nude women on calendars, she may have recourse on the grounds of sexual harassment. Although some object on grounds that such a requirement is overly intrusive (Bernstein, 1995), the intent is to maintain an environment where performance and opportunities for advancement are not impaired because of race or gender.

Affirmative action may also include targeted goals for the hiring of women and minorities. "Targeted goals" may simply involve requiring that good-faith efforts be made to to identify, select, and train potentially qualified minorities and women. However, given blatant and long-term discrimination, targeted goals may require quotas for hiring or promoting minorities and women.

Quotas and guidelines are related, but there are important differences between them. Whereas both set targets on hiring members of minority groups or women, the latter is sensitive to means and procedures, and the former, to goals and results. Under a quota system an agency or a court may *mandate* that an industry hire a certain proportion of women or minority workers. However, courts may serve a more permissive role. They may, for example, simply *allow* an enterprise to set up a quota for hiring and promoting minorities if it has an acceptable reason for doing so—say, in order to correct for present imbalances or past discrimination.

Under a system of guidelines an industry will be required to examine its hiring standards and its training procedures to assure that members of minority groups are not excluded arbitrarily from certain positions. This may entail that traditional instruments for selecting people be placed under scrutiny and evaluated in terms of their relevance to the job in question. Under a system of guidelines, a manufacturing company may, for example, set different norms for men and women on mechanical aptitude tests on the grounds that men usually have more experience with machinery than women and this experience provides them with an advantage on the test that will not necessarily translate into better performance on the shop floor. Given gendered norms, the company will probably hire more women than it otherwise would have done.

Affirmative action policies within universities are similar to those found in the work place. The actual exercise of affirmative action policy in the university may include many different features. These range from the relatively noncontroversial concern to seek out women and minority candidates to apply for positions to more controversial programs like targets-of-opportunity programs, which provide resources to departments for opening positions when a qualified woman or minority individual is available and programs that seek to readjust standards to allow more women or minorities to qualify for positions.

The military academies readjust standards when they allow women to do certain exercise routines differently than men and a law school does so when it grants admission to some African-American applicants even though their test scores may be lower than some unsuccessful White applicants. These are controversial programs, but they are usually justified on the grounds that the standards were established with certain groups in mind and that different factors may weigh as heavily in predicting the on-job performance of members of other groups.

A BRIEF HISTORY OF AFFIRMATIVE ACTION

Affirmative action legislation was initiated when it became clear that action undertaken to end discrimination, such as *Brown* v. *Board of Education* (1954), which ended legalized school segregation, was not sufficient to end exclusion. In response to pressure from civil rights organizations, a string of executive orders, court rulings, and voluntary practices was initiated in the 1960s and 1970s that was intended to address this failing, including, of course, the use of court-ordered busing to end de facto segregation in schools.

The *Brown* decision was based on the view that forced segregation was inherently unequal, that it violated the equal protection clause of the constitution, and that each citizen has a right to "be treated by organized society as a respected, responsible and participating member" (Karst, 1977, p. 4). However, as significant as forced segregation was in maintaining inequality, it was not the only factor, and Blacks were not the only group that suffered from presumptions of inferiority. For example, in education, children with disabilities have often been denied the full benefits of public education on the grounds that they were not capable of taking full advantage of them. Now laws provide children with disabilities support that helps them participate in public education.

Affirmative action officially began with Title VII of the Civil Rights Act of 1964, which prohibited discrimination on the basis of race and sex and which was later augmented by a number of executive orders that regulated federal contracts and set goals and timetables for hiring minorities. Although 1964 is usually given as the official date of the beginning of affirmative action, the idea of affirmative action goes back to an even earlier period. In 1959 then Vice-president Nixon chaired the President's Committee on Government Contracts and called for remedial steps to increase the number of Blacks hired by government contractors. Subsequently both Presidents Kennedy and Johnson issued executive orders intended to achieve nondiscrimination in federal contracts. In 1964 President Johnson signed the Civil Rights Act, which included Title VII as an instrument to end discrimination by large private employers even if they did not have government contracts (Stephanopoulos & Edley, 1995).

Many of these efforts could be described as bipartisan. In 1969 President Nixon and his labor secretary, George Shultz, issued an order to increase the meager 1.6% minority representation in the construction trades in Philadelphia by taking special measures to assure equal opportunity. Later Nixon remarked about his order:

> A good job is as basic and important a civil right as a good education. . . . I felt that the plan Shultz devised, which would require such [affirmative] action by law, was both necessary and right. We would not impose quotas, but would require federal contractors to show Affirmative Action to meet the goals of increasing minority employment. (Quoted in Stephanopoulos & Edley, 1995, p. 11)

In 1973, the Nixon administration allowed that specific hiring goals and timetables were appropriate ways to advance the national commitment to equal employment opportunity, and, not incidentally, they were also viewed as an effective strategy for dividing the different constituencies of the Democratic party (Duster, 1996).

The issue of quotas has been one of the focal points of the affirmative action debate in recent times, but the mandating of quotas by the administration or the courts has been relatively rare and has usually been ordered in response to some gross and visible discrimination. For example, in 1970 a district court ordered Alabama to end discrimination against Blacks in the hiring of state police (Alabama had never hired a Black state trooper). When, after 18 months, Alabama had still not hired a Black state police trooper, the court ordered that one qualified Black be hired for each White until 25% of the force was African-American (*NAACP* v. *Allen*, 1974). Again, in 1975 a federal district court, after finding a long history of discriminatory practices by the Sheet Metal Workers union against nonwhite workers, established a membership goal of 29% minority workers, a goal that was in proportion to the estimated minority job pool. The finding was upheld by the Supreme Court (*Local 28 of the Sheet Metal Workers* v. *E.E.O.C.*, 1986).

Although *mandating* quotas has been relatively rare, the Court has upheld voluntary plans developed by firms and their unions to hire and promote minority workers. Thus, Kaiser Aluminum and its union in Gramercy, Louisiana, cooperated on a plan to compensate for the exclusion of Black craft workers by selecting Blacks for 50% of its trainee slots until the percentage of Black craft workers in the plant matched that of the local labor pool, a practice that was upheld when later challenged in the Supreme Court (*United Steelworkers of America, AFL-CIO-CLC* v. *Weber*, 1979). These plans have been developed voluntarily as a response to a long history of exclusion and discrimination.

In some cases the Court has upheld voluntary preferential hiring even when the program is not intended to compensate for past discrimination by the enterprise. For example, the Court upheld the validity of a preferential promotion plan favoring women by the Transportation Agency in Santa Clara County (*Johnson* v. *Transportation Agency Santa Clara County, Ca.*, 1987).

In his majority opinion, Justice Brennan argued that the plan should be approved even if there was no proof that the employer had discriminated against women in the past. His argument is based on the fact that strong social pressure in the past often inhibited women from pursuing certain kinds of jobs. By definition, if women have not applied for positions, they are not directly discriminated against when men are hired to fill them. Here the majority of the Court thus allows for gender to be taken into account when doing so will probably result in a change in social attitudes that will enable a more equitable distribution of positions, and it allows this even if the attitudes supporting the earlier distribution were shared by women and men alike. As Rosenfeld (1991) writes:

> There may be strong support for the view that social attitudes which tend to channel women away from certain jobs are not only as pernicious as first-order discrimination, but in one sense even more harmful. Whereas first-order discrimination is generally manifest for all to see, and its effects well known, the evils attributable to sexist social attitudes are often concealed, and their effects not readily perceived even by their victims. Accordingly, the evil consequences of sexist social attitudes may be easier to perpetuate than those of first order discrimination. (p. 200)

In recent years, the Court has taken a more restrictive attitude toward voluntary affirmative action programs in which companies hire or advance Blacks or women over those White men who by conventional standards are more qualified. Here the company must show that it had practiced such discrimination. And, in a recent finding, the Court has held that many federal affirmative action programs must meet a higher test and show a compelling state interest in requiring and enforcing affirmative action standards (*Adarand Constructors, Inc.* v. *Pena*, 1995). The enforcement of "strict standards" places a stronger burden of proof on those who seek to advance the case of affirmative action by requiring, for example, a close link between those who claim affirmative action benefits and those who have been the victims of discrimination. The requirement of "tailored means" directs that race-neutral remedies should be considered and, if available, are preferable to race-targeted ones. Hence, under the idea of tailored means, it is preferable to aid Black business through special programs to help all small businesses in an area where Blacks comprise a sizable proportion of the business population rather than through programs exclusively targeted to Black enterprises. The tailored-means test does not require that the former course always be chosen, but it does require that it be considered and rejected only if it will not be adequate in aiding Black business (*City of Richmond* v. *J. A. Croson*, 1989).

AFFIRMATIVE ACTION AND HIGHER EDUCATION

University admissions was not an early target of affirmative action, but it has become one through litigation and administrative interpretation of existing laws. Given the importance of colleges and universities in supplying and renewing the nation's managerial and professional labor force, the extension of affirmative action enforcement to universities is perfectly reasonable. Despite their alleged liberal proclivities, both the student body and the faculty at most selective universities and most of the higher prestige and income producing professional programs have been largely white and largely male. In the late 1960s colleges and universities began to take steps to increase the percentage of Blacks and women in their programs. These programs have succeeded in increasing the enrollment of women, Blacks, and other targeted minorities. Whereas in 1955 at the dawn of the Civil Rights Movement Black enrollment in colleges and universities comprised 4.9% of college age students (18–24), by 1990 the percentage of Black students had risen to 11.3%. Women, who now comprise 50% of all college students, showed similar gains in both undergraduate and professional programs (Stephanopoulos & Edley, 1995). Since the late 1970s many of the more aggressive programs have come under attack and a comparison of the recent order by the University of California Regents, mentioned at the beginning of this chapter, with past actions of that same body illustrates just how dramatic this shift has been.

In 1978 the Regents stood as the defendant in a case brought by Allan Bakke, a White applicant, who claimed that the University of California Medical School at the Davis campus had discriminated against him in granting admission to Black applicants with lower scores (*Regents of the University of California* v. *Bakke*, 1978). The U.S. Supreme Court, in a highly politicized split decision, ruled that the university's admission procedure violated Bakke's rights and rejected the university's procedure of setting aside a specific number of slots for minorities.

The opinion of Justice Powell, generally accepted as providing the bridging opinion between the differing justices, marks a turning point in the history of affirmative action. Instead of supporting voluntary efforts to increase minority enrollment as the Court would still do in the 1979 Kaiser Aluminum case (*United Steelworkers* v. *Weber*, 1979), in *Bakke* the Court prohibited the university from using race as a criterion for setting aside spaces and allowed only that it be considered as part of a larger diversity standard such as region of the country.

Although Black enrollment as a percentage of college students has continued to increase somewhat since *Bakke* (from 9.1% in 1980 to 11.3% in 1990), there has been considerable backsliding in terms of the proportion of Black 18–24-year-old high school graduates attending college. Stephanopoulos writes,

> Through the availability of student aid programs and aggressive recruitment and retention programs, the college-going rate for blacks and whites who graduate from high school was about equal by 1977. Since 1977, however, the proportion of black 18–24 year old high school graduates enrolled in college has not kept pace with that of white students. While the percentage of black students who have graduated from high school has increased approximately 20 percent in the past 25 years, the portion of black high school student graduates attending college is now 25 percent less than that of white students. (Stephanopoulos & Edley, pp. 12–13)

While one may either applaud the fact that more African-American students are graduating from high school or decry the fact that a smaller percentage of this total are attending college, since *Bakke* the trend in education, as elsewhere, has been greater scrutiny of race- and gender-based affirmative action programs. It is likely that this trend contributes to the decline in the relative proportion of Black high school graduates attending college.

Bakke precipitated three important changes in education. The first is that universities and professional schools are not expected to address the consequences of larger historical discrimination. Rather, according to Powell's opinion, they must do so only insofar as they advance another goal–group diversity for the purpose of educational enrichment. The second is that "diversity" entails neutrality with regard to the preferred group. It may be used to target historically oppressed minorities, but then, in theory, it is possible for schools to find members of other groups more enriching for the student body as a whole. Third, advancing the goal of diversity is now a voluntary, not a compulsory, matter for colleges and universities.

By ignoring the historical basis of affirmative action, *Bakke* began the shift away from race- and gender-based affirmative action that we are witnessing today. This shift has continued, not only in the recent order by the Regents of the University of California but by the rejection by the U.S. Fifth Circuit Court of Appeals of a special program at the University of Texas designed to increase the number of Black and Hispanic law school students (*Hopwood* v. *Texas*, 1996).

In issuing its opinion, this court exposed the weakness in Powell's argument by correctly noting that there is no viewpoint that essentially belongs to one race or gender. It thus rejected Powell's argument that using race to achieve a diverse student body is a compelling state interest. Citing the rejection of Powell's argument by other justices in the *Bakke* case, this finding by the Fifth District court (which the U.S. Supreme Court refused to review) continued to narrow the grounds on which affirmative action admissions could be developed, and citing *Croson*, the District Court affirmed that the law school's attempt to remedy past injustices went beyond reasonable limits (*Hopwood* v. *Texas*, 1996). The rejection of diversity as an adequate standard when coupled with the strict standards narrows the window for affirmative action remedies even while admitting the enormity of past discrimination. As the majority opinion in *Hopwood* declared:

> The case against race-based preferences does not rest on the sterile assumption that American society is untouched or unaffected by the tragic oppression of its past. Rather, it is the very enormity of that tragedy that lends resolve to the desire never to repeat it, and find a legal order in which distinctions based on race shall have no place. (Opinion of Jerry E. Smith in *Hopwood* v. *Texas* 1996)

While recognizing the enormity of the tragedy, the court ironically disabled the university's program for addressing it. Although the general principle used to support this ruling is flawed, the court is, as I argue subsequently, correct in its rejection of diversity as a compelling state interest. Yet, as I will show in Chapter 4, the case for affirmative action is considerably more compelling than either *Bakke* or *Hopwood* allows.

RECENT ATTACKS ON AFFIRMATIVE ACTION

Recent political attacks on affirmative action have depended to a large extent on highlighting certain episodic practices and rulings, each of which may be debated on its own terms. However, these attacks do not add up to an adequate refutation of the justifications that support affirmative action, and their persuasive force largely depends on distorting the basic reasons for affirmative action.

An adequate refutation of race- and gender-based affirmative action could come only after a full and reasonable evaluation of the justifications themselves. Rather than accept this responsibility, many of the critics of affirmative action believe that if they simply add up "negative" cases of its application, it will fall of its own weight (Bolick, 1996; Eastland, 1996).

This way of arguing has at least two problems. First, there are few policies that do not aid some accidental and undeserving beneficiary. For example, the Tennessee Valley Authority (TVA) was set up during the Roosevelt administration to aid the people in Appalachia because of its low level of development and its poverty. Nevertheless, the dams and generating plants that were developed in the region aided both rich and poor. Second, arguments against affirmative action often neglect the historical and social contexts in which decisions about affirmative action are made. For example, Eastland (1996), in arguing against a race-based policy for minorities, dismisses as irrelevant the argument of its early proponents that at the time minorities "had won less than one per cent of all federal procurement while minorities made up between 15 and 18 percent of the general population" (p. 120). He argues that (1) because no member of Congress had identified any specific wrong and (2) because no evidence was presented that any of the firms that would benefit from the program were the objects of discrimination or that (3) no evidence was provided that any of the firms that would be obliged to subcontract had actually discriminated, then the requirement was unfair. He writes that "it did not matter to Congress that the set-aside, in remedying discrimination practiced by no one in particular, would benefit minority businesses regardless of whether or not they had actually experienced discrimination in procurement" (p. 121).

Eastland's assumption that there is a need to prove historical discrimination against Blacks on a case-by-case basis could be persuasive only to the historically illiterate or the politically irresponsible. Recent court cases notwithstanding, in cases of African Americans the burden needs to be shifted and those who wish to deny the benefits of affirmative action for a given program must be able to show why, in this particular case, past discrimination need not be taken into account.

To hold that nothing is owed to a Black-owned firm unless there has been specific acts of *proven* discrimination against it and that nothing is owed by a White-owned firm unless it has actually practiced discrimination is the equivalent of distributing prizes in a race according to who crosses the finish line first without regard to whether the runners have completed a 26-mile marathon or a 100-yard dash.

Since the Civil War, while Black-owned firms were being discriminated against in the construction and other industries, White-owned firms were building up capital, developing contacts, establishing reputations, and developing new techniques and skills. Had Black-owned firms been allowed to compete on equal grounds during this time, all else being reasonably equal, many of these advantages would have been leveled and special consideration would not be required.

Certainly it is important, as Eastland (1996) suggests, to understand the reasons for any present distribution of benefits before we know whether a reallocation of some sort is justified. However, it is a flawed historical memory that operates on the assumption that African Americans have to prove that they have been victimized by discrimination.

THE NEED FOR A THEORY
OF AFFIRMATIVE ACTION

Affirmative action began with one group in mind—African Americans—but it has been expanded to address the concerns of other groups as well. The original model has thus had to accommodate itself to other concerns without addressing the core question—what it is that should allow some but not all people to advance claims on the basis of their identity as members of a certain group. When affirmative action encompassed only one group—African Americans—it was clear and obvious that the projects were a response not only to present equalities, but to the historical conditions that created them. Eastland (1996) and other conservative critics can conveniently forget this only because other groups have entered the arena with different experiences that require different models to understand. History may play a role in the claims that all of these groups make for consideration under affirmative action, but it will not be the same history and it will not work in the same way. Think, for example, of the different reasons for affirmative action that might be used to justify its application to people with disabilities, as opposed to those appropriate for justifying the claims of African-American people.

Moreover, the issue of affirmative action is confusing because of its partial success. When people notice the growth in the Black middle class and the increased percentage of Black professionals (especially prior to the *Bakke* decision); when they are told that in Black middle-class households where there are two parents income reached parity with whites in similar situations (this is a decreasing proportion of the total Black families), they begin to feel that the job has been accomplished. Yet this not only assumes that affirmative action is primarily involved with income and poverty, it also overlooks the uneven face of progress even in these areas. In some of the most important measures, the discrepancy is huge. For example, Duster (1996) reports that "in 1991, the median net worth of White households ($43,279) was more than *ten times* that of the median net worth of African American households ($4,169)" (p. 45). Of course one must factor in such things as whether the household is headed by a woman, whether there are two parents present, and so forth. However, these are not just additional variables; they are also general indexes of well-being that have enormous socioeconomic significance and are reflected in homicide rates and low male and infant life expectancy.

Even though affirmative action programs were initiated largely in response to concerns raised by the Civil Rights Movement and to the historical injustices imposed on African Americans as a result of slavery and discrimination, they have proved equally important in addressing the concerns of women. The increase in the divorce rate, the growing number of women in the work force, the income gap between genders, and changing ideas about gender-marked work highlight the needs of women in both education and employment. Moreover, the emphasis by Justice Powell on the importance of diversity and his reluctance to continue to provide a singular special importance to race coincided with increasing immigration from Asia and South America. This lent support to the view that affirmative action should apply to all people of color.

These changes, together with the grafting of affirmative action onto a number of debates initiated by feminism and postmodernism, have created an array of different opinions about the purpose and goals of the policy. As Hollinger (1996) nicely puts it:

> Some acquaintances tell me that Affirmative Action is good because it promotes cultural diversity within the student body and the faculty. Others ridicule this argument as an example of ethno-racial essentialism, carrying the expectation that culture follows blood. My most adamantly antiessentialist friends make the case for campus Affirmative Action on a wholly different basis: A need to expand the middle class within certain demographic blocs whose members, because of a prejudice triggered by the physical characteristics that serve to identify these blocs, have been historically prevented from achieving upward mobility. (p. 31)

Hollinger rightly holds that these differences call for a theory of affirmative action.

In my mind such a theory must be able to do a number of different things. First, it must be able to account for the basic ethical intuitions that support the general idea that members of some groups require special consideration. In other words it must address the issue of whether affirmative action is a group right and whether, if it is, it can be allowed in societies that promote the idea of individual merit. Second, it must account for some of the different ethical intuitions that lead different groups of people to claim that they are owed such consideration. Third, it must allow for some sense of how priorities may be established between these different claims. Finally, it must begin to understand the place that affirmative action itself should have in theories of a just society. It is also important for such a theory to be able to draw some boundaries around appropriate affirmative action policies and to distinguish them from other reform efforts.

In this book I defend race- and gender-based affirmative action policies against attempts to eliminate them entirely, as many conservatives would like to do, or to replace them by programs that focus on economic need rather than on race and gender, as some liberals as well as some conservatives are proposing. The argument that I offer is that affirmative action programs that are designed to improve the position of women and certain minorities are, in principle, morally acceptable remedies to certain forms of unjustified inequalities, and these inequalities will not be adequately addressed if the problems are redefined in economic terms alone or by programs that seek only diversity. If this argument is successful it will have contributed to the development of a theory of affirmative action.

Before developing such a theory, it is important to note that there are a number of alternative forms of affirmative action that have recently been proposed. Many of these advocate shifting the ground of affirmative action from a race- and gender-based policy to a need-based one. Here economic class and need rather than race and gender would constitute the target category of affirmative action, and special consideration would be given to people because they are poor rather than because they are Black, Hispanic, or women. This alternative has obvious political and some ethical appeal. However, I do not believe that it can serve as an adequate substitute for a race- and gender-based approach, and in Chapter 3 I show why.

A SKETCH OF THE CENTRAL ARGUMENT

I argue that race- and gender-based affirmative action is designed to improve the position of targeted minorities and women and is a morally acceptable and desirable remedy to certain forms of unjustified inequalities. Briefly my argument in this book is as follows:

Critics of affirmative action wrongly believe that it is unfair and morally inadequate because it advances people on the basis of their membership in groups rather than on the basis of their individual merit. Thus these critics think that affirmative action violates accepted notions of individual rights and equal opportunity, substituting in their place a morally questionable notion of group rights. In contrast I show that affirmative action has three morally defensible goals and that the means by which it addresses these are also morally permissible. First, it seeks to correct systematic and long-standing ruptures in the exercise of the principle of equal opportunity. Second, it seeks to advance the standing of people who have been discriminated against because of certain ascribed characteristics such as gender or skin color. Third, it attempts to address a historical obligation. I conclude that while affirmative action is, at least in principle, an adequate moral response for advancing the first two goals, it is a necessary but not sufficient response for addressing the third.

Throughout much of this book I note that affirmative action should not be mistaken for programs that seek to advance other socially desirable goals such as the reduction of poverty or the promotion of diversity. In the last chapter I argue that these goals should play a role in affirmative action policy, but not a primary one. I also show how the implications for affirmative action may be different for different groups of people.

CHAPTER 2

Markets, Measurement, and Affirmative Action

To its critics, affirmative action stands as an inefficient substitute for the more rational market processes of selection. According to this view, when market forces are left to operate on their own without interference from externally imposed ideas of fairness, enterprises that fail to hire the most talented candidates, regardless of race, gender, or class, will fail. Accordingly, if race and gender are short-run considerations and are allowed to interrupt market selection, according to these critics, they will result in long-term distortions and inefficiencies.

In this chapter I analyze this criticism and show why it is inadequate. I argue that advocates of market selection have a large burden to show that existing inequalities have less to do with racism, sexism, or other forms of injustice than they do with the tendency of market mechanisms to select for the most efficient traits. I show that the market criticism is valid only if one holds to a questionable conception of intelligence, one most recently expressed in the book *The Bell Curve* (Herrnstein & Murray, 1994).

After addressing some of the problems involved in this conception of intelligence, I briefly examine a criticism of a different order. Here the critic is concerned not with the inefficiency of affirmative action, but with its inability to address the problems of the poor. I agree with this critic that affirmative action may function well even while poverty persists and possibly even intensifies. However, I show that even though affirmative action is not to be justified primarily as an antipoverty program, its conception of fairness is still important to pursue.

THE MARKET AS A FAIR SELECTOR— PROBLEMS WITH THE THEORY

Some who oppose affirmative action do so because they reject any government intervention in the market, including the academic market of talent, on the grounds that it promotes inefficiency. They hold that any progress in advancing women and minorities will come through the private sentiments of individuals and the voluntary activities of business in response to market forces rather than through government intervention. They believe that affirmative action is self-defeating because the inefficiencies that it creates lead to a reduced standard of living for all. The argument is seductive because it suggests that very little is needed to empower individuals who now are the beneficiaries of elaborate affirmative action rules. Epstein (1995), one of the most persuasive proponents of this view, believes that the prevailing sentiment for diversity is so great that "the strong hand of government is not needed to give women and minorities a boost" (p. 180).

This view is overly optimistic and there is little, either in terms of the soundness of the theory or the adequacy of the empirical evidence, to support the belief that comparable levels of change will necessarily occur without government regulation. Indeed there is considerable reason to support the opposite conclusion—that when firms are subject to affirmative action review and enforcement, the employment of minorities and women increases (Leonard, 1984, 1990).

Although there is a connection between public sentiment and industrial hiring and promotion practices, it is not, as Epstein seems to believe, that all of a sudden sentiments change in some magical, mystical way and that without prodding individual firms begin to realize their social responsibility and to hire great numbers of minorities and women. They change because people who have been denied positions because of race or gender and their sympathizers begin to pressure business, and government and education agencies. As these groups become more vocal and active about discrimination against them, the attitude of the public at large, tacitly supportive of the status quo, divides into at least three segments. Some want to maintain things as they are, others support the demands for change on moral or other grounds, and still others seek a settlement hoping that their lives will return to relative peace and quiet.

Epstein is the latest in a line of theorists (Banfield, 1970; Herrnstein & Murray, 1994) who believe that market forces alone are sufficient to correct for discrimination in the work place, and that affirmative action serves only to distort market processes. They believe the market is sufficiently supple to allow shifts in sentiment to be disciplined by "painful marginal calculations of how much they can have of a good thing before it becomes a bad thing" (Epstein, 1995, p. 180). The "good thing" includes hiring too many people who look like you.

Hence, the manager of a firm who hires only white men will supposedly find himself at a disadvantage if his competitors begin to hire more talented women and minorities, and this disadvantage will either require that he too widen his search for talent or begin to lose profits. Yet, should this not really happen, Epstein has a way to both explain it and to save the good reputation of the market. There are, after all, many practices that appear to be discriminatory but, when scrutinized adequately, prove to be otherwise.

Epstein argues, for example, that policies that seek equal pay for equal work among men and women often ignore collateral costs for different types of workers and hence distort important market considerations. If, for example, a woman can work at the same pace as a man on an assembly line but is prone to a higher rate of injury, then the true cost of labor must be weighed, according to Epstein, in terms of the cost of injuries as well as the output of goods. And if the cost of a woman worker is higher than that of a male, then the firm actually discriminates against men when it overlooks this cost and hires women at the same wage. The result also militates against women, by making employers more reluctant to hire them because of the real premium that must be paid if they are to receive the same wages as men.

Epstein's argument ignores instances in which the market serves to reward cases of discrimination. Imagine that the work force in factories in the United States that produce widgets is White and male and that the culture in each of these enterprises is racist and sexist. Suppose too that there are some women who would make widgets equally as well as, and would cost no more than, the present workers under nonsexist conditions. However, under sexist conditions they get nervous, perhaps even irritated, possibly angry, and as a result, their productivity falters; they produce fewer widgets and have more accidents. Moreover, women's presence on the shop floor violates the men's ideas of fit and appropriateness, and they continue to make life uncomfortable for female workers. Suppose that when women leave because of such harassment, the men's morale and productivity increase.

Given this situation, any one firm that hires women is at a significant disadvantage. If it chose to change its sexist culture, it would have to absorb the cost of doing so and would thus have an expense that a less enlightened factory would not have. If it chose to allow the women to work without changing the culture, then it would have to put up with a slower, less efficient work force, and again it would be at a competitive disadvantage. Of course, it may be acceptable to Epstein that the women be paid less even though the cause of their higher cost is outside of their control and is the result of historical discrimination. Epstein might argue that nervousness, irritation, and anger, even if provoked, should be controlled, and that if a worker's productivity suffers as a result, she should be replaced. However, to make this argument stick, he needs more than market economics. He needs, among other things, a conception of human nature in which moral responsibility resides in the person provoked rather than with those who are doing the provoking.

Epstein also ignores the fact that the market *as it is*, as opposed to some ideal in the heads of theorists, also encourages companies to take advantage of discriminatory cultural practices. Because of cultural assumptions that women belong at home, taking care of children, companies can hire men without providing day care for children.

Epstein is able to maintain this optimistic view of market forces and "cultural fairness" because (with regard to the question of affirmative action) he treats the single firm as the unit of analysis and underemphasizes the dynamics of the field created by the firms' interactions with each other. Indeed, were every manager of every firm an enlightened feminist, the dynamics of the field would require that many reforms be rejected unless there could be some assurance that every firm would act under the same set of rules.

Suppose, to use Epstein's example of safety, that the reason for the greater number of accidents among women workers was that the factory was designed with the anatomy and physical requirements of men in mind, and that, given this design, unless all competitors were required to make the kind of changes that would accommodate women, any single factory that did so would be at a competitive disadvantage. Under these circumstances the only way to achieve the ideal of providing people of equal merit with reasonably similar opportunities and rewards is to mandate new safety requirements for all competitors.

Affirmative action seeks similarly to allow virtuous action by providing an even playing field for doing the right thing. The government requires that every widget factory make good-faith efforts to hire and retain women. The role of government should also be to see that such steps are taken to level the international playing field as well so that when domestic companies do the right thing they are not undercut by foreign competitors who do the wrong thing. In too many instances, however, international trade treaties have neglected this obligation.

The belief that the market is the best way to advance members of stigmatized groups is plausible because those who advocate free markets and those who seek nondiscrimination are both driven by a concern to eliminate irrelevant distinctions—distinctions that are accidents of birth and that do not affect performance. Race, sex, religious belief, and ethnicity are often cited as examples of irrelevant distinctions by both those who advance the cause of stigmatized groups and those who advance the cause of free markets. There are differences, though, in the way in which the market advocates and the affirmative action advocates think about irrelevant characteristics, and these differences are sufficient to disrupt the initial plausibility of a coincidence of interest.

First, whereas many advocates of affirmative action hold that attending to race and sex in the short run will lead to race- and sex-free selection in the long run, the advocates of market selection believe that if race and sex are short-run considerations, they will result in long-term distortions and inefficiencies. Market advocates hold that in both the short and the long term the market can provide for fair selection. The trick, they believe, is to eliminate present discrimination (including what they view as "discrimination" against White males), not to compensate for past discrimination.

Second, there is an important difference in the priority that race-and-gender affirmative action advocates and market advocates place on nondiscrimination. Advocates of markets seek first efficiency and low cost, and in doing so, they must allow for the possibility that race or gender bias may affect production in a positive way. Given their commitment to market efficiency, they must also allow that if such circumstances arise, discrimination is permissible.

Consider a factory in which owners, managers, and workers belong to the same ethnic group and where, as a result, certain conflicts that occur in other similar factories are absent here. Given this higher level of cultural uniformity, the company is more efficient than its competitors and seeks to maintain that efficiency by hiring from the same ethnic group. Because cultural uniformity is a factor in the efficiency of this plant and ultimately in its profits, many strong advocates of market reform would believe the hiring practices justified.

Advocates of affirmative action view such an advantage differently. They hold that the hiring practices are wrong, even if they do increase the firm's efficiency, and that the fact that they provide the firm with advantages over those that seek fairness makes them even more so. Some will argue for this concept of affirmative action in terms only of past discrimination—culturally generated efficiency is wrong when it is a product of past discrimination; others will argue it on present and future terms—it is wrong because it continues to bestow undeserved advantages and disadvantages and inhibits the development of talent. These differences are important, but whichever way one argues the case for affirmative action, market efficiency is rejected as the ultimate determinant of policy. For most advocates of affirmative action, efficiency is constrained by a certain conception of fairness in educational and employment selection. It is a conception in which a disadvantage that arises out of past injustice must be addressed even if doing so is not maximally efficient.

THE PROBLEM WITH THE EMPIRICAL EVIDENCE: MARKET EFFICIENCY AND EDUCATIONAL SELECTION

Even if efficiency is accepted as the primary value, the advocates of market selection have a large burden to show that existing inequalities have less to do with racism, sexism, or other forms of injustice than with the tendency of market mechanisms to select for the most efficient traits. Without some independent point of validation, their claim is suspect. It seems to say that whatever the market selects is what we will *define* as maximally efficient.

Yet in a world in which patterns of wealth and poverty as well as education are very different for different groups, this burden is difficult to lift. The problem is that if a great deal of talent is hidden because of educational discrimination—as seems likely—then the existing distribution of positions and rewards will appear fair even though, under some other possible educational system, there would actually be a higher level of performance and greater workplace efficiency.

The opposing view—that existing inequalities are not the result of the suppression of hidden talents and unequal educational opportunities—is argued by Herrnstein and Murray (1994). They contend that IQ tests provide an independent measure for efficient selection and they argue that such tests show that American education, with the exception of affirmative action selection, is doing a more efficient job than ever of sorting children into programs that are appropriate to their intellectual talents. They argue that highly selective colleges and universities are selecting, teaching, and placing into the most important and highest-paying jobs the most talented of America's youth and that they are doing so in greater proportion to their numbers in the general population than ever before. As a result, America is becoming more of a meritocracy than it ever was before, and an increasing number of intelligent people are being placed in demanding colleges and in highly rewarding jobs. As Scarr observes, Herrnstein and Murray believe that more and more of the pathology in American society is related to low intelligence (Scarr, 1995) and that this is so even as the patterns of racial inequality remain relatively unbroken. The cause of most of the remaining racial inequality in society, they suggest, is a stubborn and largely unchangeable difference in intelligence, a difference in which race and genetics play a sizable role.

Herrnstein and Murray believe that affirmative action programs are bound to fail because they insist on advancing less qualified Black students and workers over more qualified White ones. The argument, if correct, supports the idea that test scores and grades are more efficient selectors for college and professional school and that market selection is a more efficient and fairer way than affirmative action to allocate jobs. As one commentator puts it: "They suggest that affirmative action has the effect of reducing the opportunity for the nation to achieve its potential because it exercises artificial constraints upon some people's cognitive ability" (Nettles, 1995, p. 17). Equal opportunity will not produce equal outcomes when people differ in their intellectual capacities. Nor will equal opportunity produce equal educational outcomes for different races if the members of the racial groups display, as an aggregate, differing and unequal intellectual capacities (Gottfredson, 1992).

The research reported in *The Bell Curve* (Herrnstein & Murray, 1994) is not new and, in its different incarnations, has been the subject of significant challenges on both empirical and conceptual grounds (Block & Dworkin, 1974a, b; Feinberg, 1983; Gould, 1994). The underlying belief that intelligence can be measured on an ordinal scale is an example of misplaced precision, similar, say, to the idea that we can assign meaningful numbers to goodness. Dewey captured the problem of misplaced precision with the following anecdote:

> Listening to these papers I was reminded of the way we used to weigh hogs on the farm. We would put a plank in between the rails of the fence, put the hog on one end of the plank and then pile up the other end of the plank with rocks until the rocks balanced the hog. Then we took the hog off; and then we guessed the weight of the rocks. (Quoted in Bredo, 1995, p. 2)

Dewey would be generous if he applied his example to the research in *The Bell Curve*, for at least he knew what it was he was attempting to weigh—the hog. What is being measured when we measure "intelligence" is considerably less clear and certainly less uniform (Gardner, 1993).

Herrnstein and Murray (1994) believe that an intelligence test measures our capacity to learn, and they also believe that a considerable portion of this capacity is genetically grounded and thus not subject to change through education or environmental manipulation. It is this belief that leads them to reject, against good evidence to the contrary (Schweinhart, Barnes, & Weikart, 1993; Schweinhart & Weikart, 1986a, b), many social programs, such as Head Start, as inherently ineffective and others, such as affirmative action, as inefficient. Cognitive ability is just something that cannot be influenced. Their argument, as Gould (1994) notes, rests

> on the validity of four shaky premises, all asserted (but hardly discussed or defended) by Herrnstein and Murray. Intelligence, in their formulation,

> must be depictable as a single number, capable of ranking people in linear order, genetically based, and effectively immutable. If any of these premises are false, their entire argument collapses. For example, if all are true except immutability, then programs for early intervention in education might work to boost I. Q. permanently, just as a pair of eyeglasses may correct a defect in vision. The central argument of "The Bell Curve" fails because most of the premises are false. (p. 139)

There are other problems with *The Bell Curve*. The authors assume, for example, that "Black" and "White" refer to genetically uniform groups when there is more in-group variation than between-group variation in terms of DNA. As Marks (1995) notes:

> The biological differences between groups are trifling compared to those within the group, and . . . the major biological divisions of humans presumed to be "out there" do not manifest themselves clearly. Race doesn't explain the patterns of diversity of human behavior; and ultimately even simple classifications of races emerge to be based more on cultural perceptions of who-is-more-like-whom than on biological criteria. (p. 261)

Herrnstein and Murray (1994) believe that they have shown the futility of educational intervention with an argument that most of the gains in IQ scores achieved through programs like Head Start wash out as children progress through elementary school. However, they make this claim without any examination of the quality of the elementary school or the home life of the children (Nettles, 1995, p. 16). Herrnstein and Murray say virtually nothing meaningful about the intervening variables of school practice or family life that might be used to explain different patterns of performance among different groups, nor do they explore the different beliefs about authority and trust that might affect performance at school and work (McDermott, 1982; Ogbu, 1991).

What we count as a high level of competence depends to a certain extent on what we, as a society, want. For example, when women and nonwhite men were largely excluded from medical school (partly because of test scores, but also because of the general social climate that such test scores reflected), research on diseases that affected these groups was neglected without any great outcry from within the profession. Society would have been better off under such circumstances to select for more gender and racial diversity even if it meant a higher investment in initial training costs. To argue for efficient selection on the basis of an initial input/output model alone neglects instances in which additional wider selection criteria, even with higher training costs, will enhance efficiency.

When the instruments for "measuring" the quality of results are as vague and biased as IQ tests, the problem is compounded.

Many other aspects of the argument are problematic as well. There is the question of whether it is meaningful to attribute higher or lower intelligence to groups, rather than individuals. To hold that it is rests on the belief that it is possible to develop a test that is culture fair. However, actual so-called culture-fair tests, which tend to show larger differences between Blacks and Whites than more "culture-loaded tests," depend largely on the development of specific spatial skills (Feinberg, 1983), and as Sternberg (1985) notes:

> Unfortunately, people's experiences with tasks and classes of tasks tend to differ widely across cultures (and even, to a fairly large extent, within cultures). I doubt whether tests can be precisely equated in terms of the extent to which they measure . . . across different groups. (p. 77)

The argument also rests on the belief that the claim "IQ tests measure intelligence" is unambiguous in its meaning when in fact the meaning of the claim is unclear (Feinberg, 1983). It could mean that skills and concepts are arranged in a hierarchy of difficulty that is basically the same for all of us and that measured intelligence will tell us just how far up the hierarchy any one of us will be able to progress. Given this unlikely meaning, then to place a person whose conceptual potential was low in a position that required acquiring higher-level skills and concepts would be wasteful. The resources spent would not achieve the results needed. This claim is, however, insupportable. Consider, for example, that the actual intellectual capacity of human beings has changed little, if at all, over the last 500 years. Yet there are innumerable concepts, understandings, and processes that most of us can now grasp that were unavailable to the most intelligent people living 500 years ago.

The more likely meaning of "IQ tests measure intelligence" is that IQ tests indicate the relative speed at which people may be expected to learn certain tasks. Certainly, if this claim is true, which it may be given equal cultural resources (a big thing to give in our society), more resources would have to be spent on those who learn more slowly if we wished them to arrive at the same point as those who are swifter learners.

However, to use speed of learning alone to measure efficiency would be shortsighted, as any manufacturer of video recorders learned many years ago, as they chose not to restrict sales to those 7-year-olds who could learn how to use their machines effortlessly. Rather, they wisely chose to design easier-to-use machines, indicating that when the task is important enough there should be a strong reason to devise better methods for teaching it to people who may, for whatever reason, take more time to learn it. To suggest otherwise is to assume a large and necessary correspondence between the speed at which a skill is learned and the adequacy with which, once learned, it will be practiced.

Putting aside the thorny issue of whether Black people and White people actually do constitute two genetically uniform groups, there is the question whether and how much measured inequality contributes to unequal achievement and positioning. For example, *The Bell Curve* (Herrnstein & Murray, 1994) notes that the largest gap between Black and White children occurs not at the lower SES levels, but at the higher ones. Oddly, the authors mention this as evidence of the fairness of the tests. However, one might better conclude that above a certain level, measured intelligence, whatever it means, need not make a large difference in achievement or position. Nevertheless, Herrnstein and Murray report this fact because they mistakenly believe that it allows them to control for environmental input—wrongly assuming that the experience of a middle-class White child and a middle-class Black child is the same.

Test scores and grades are not self-interpreting. For example, a recent study showed that women with the same grades and background as men perform less well as a group in law school. Rather than attribute this to some inherent quality in their intellect that allows men to do better than women in legal reasoning, the authors attributed the finding to the fact that law schools reflected an aggressive, maschismo culture and rewarded aggressive behavior. Rather than citing the better performance of men as a way to explain the higher status of male lawyers, the authors used the greater success of men to explore the way in which law school is experienced by women and to challenge the culture of the law school and (by implication) of the legal profession as a whole (Fine, Guinier, & Balin, 1994).

Yet the authors of *The Bell Curve* (Herrnstein & Murray, 1994) ignore the way in which home life and school are experienced by different groups of children and assume that we can understand the correlations that exist between intelligence test scores, school achievement, and economic success without understanding this difference—this in spite of the fact that there is considerable research suggesting that gender, social class, and race are critical factors in the way in which children experience life inside and outside of school (Cazden, 1989; Gilligan, 1982; Heath, 1983; McDermott, 1982; Rist, 1970).

Even if we could agree that IQ tests measure intelligence in some meaningful way, this does not tell us why children perform at the level they do in school or why certain racial and gendered patterns of inequality exist. Nor does it tell us what to do about these differences. Suppose, for example, that we assume that there is something akin to "real" intelligence and that it is related closely to the physiology or the chemistry of the brain. Perhaps imagine that certain chemicals flow faster or that there are more neurons of a certain type. (Think of a computer and the various reasons one can do more things and some things faster with one model than with another.) Something like this is probably the image of intelligence that researchers like Herrnstein and Murray have in mind. Yet this model does not tell us what we should do if we ever were able to obtain such a fine-grained understanding of different capacities. Should we arrange or pace the material differently? Should we give more attention to the slower learners? Should we correct them more? Less? Not try to teach them at all? To assume that little if anything should be done, as the authors of *The Bell Curve* appear to do, is like restricting the work of near-sighted people to tasks that require them to be only a short distance from the object when it would be more effective and humane to prescribe eyeglasses.

Whatever *The Bell Curve* and kindred studies may be about, they are not, as they pretend, a neutral guide to policy formation and they say little about the merits or the demerits of affirmative action. The authors of *The Bell Curve* obviously think otherwise, and many "free market" critics of affirmative action believe they are right.

The authors spend a considerable amount of time attempting to show that we are close to the limits of meritorious selection and that unlike the past there is but a very small overlap in intelligence between those selected for high-ranking educational institutions and those who either do not apply or who are not selected (Herrnstein & Murray, 1994, pp. 29–50), and they spend even more time discussing ethnic and racial differences in IQ (pp. 317–339) and cognitive ability (pp. 269–314). They spend no time in telling us what difference all this makes in terms of what high scorers are able to do that, with sufficient educational resources, lower scorers will not be able to do. Without this knowledge any judgment about how to expend educational resources will be sorely incomplete.

Moreover, their claim that this is a new era in American life suggests that they are unaware of the history of their own research program. From the early days of IQ testing some researchers have been claiming that tests show that the rich are rich because they are smarter and more moral and that the poor are poor because they are less intelligent and less moral. As E. L. Thorndike wrote in the early part of this century: "The natural Process which gives power to men of ability . . . are [*sic*] not, in their results, unmoral. Such men are, by and large, of superior intelligence, and consequently of somewhat superior justice and good will" (quoted in Karier, 1986, p. 19). Reading the work of these early test enthusiasts, one would think there was little room for improvement even at the turn of the century. Apparently oblivious to these earlier observations, Herrnstein and Murray believe they have shown that things just kept getting better and better.

The most harmful social aspect of studies that claim an unequal racial distribution of intelligence is the assumption that intelligence is a commodity that is distributed to individuals alone and has little to do with the way in which an enterprise is organized or the way its members interact with one another. Yet this assumption is wrong on a number of levels. Consider, for example, one of the factors motivating recent works on academic performance—the competition between the United States and Japan for economic superiority. Herrnstein and Murray allow us to conclude that the recent success of the Japanese is due to their somewhat higher IQ scores, a consideration that they pay significant attention to as a prelude to their reporting of the lower scores of African Americans.

However, most informed commentators attribute the productivity of the Japanese to the unique organization of the work place and to the fact that many different people at all levels of production are given a voice in the process (Abegglen & Stalk, 1985; Cummings, 1980; Feinberg, 1993; Vogel, 1979). There is good evidence to support this view. As American industry has reorganized in recent years, productivity has increased without any significant increase in IQ scores. This suggests that whatever individual or group limits there may be to intelligence, we have a long way to go before the potential of our present capacities is reached. It also suggests that an environment that seeks not to order intelligence from highest to lowest but to make everyone think and act smarter is what we should seek.

Intelligence involves the capacity to adapt to an established environment and to shape that environment in new ways so that it serves our needs and purposes. Since a large part of this environment consists of other people, the more understandings and information can be shared, needs and purposes coordinated, and activity mutually planned and carried out, the greater the likelihood that individual and collective goals will be met efficiently. By focusing only on individual performance, traditional IQ research simply fails to address the more important issue of how to organize an environment so that everyone's capacities are developed to their fullest.

Clearly individuals differ in what they can learn and in how fast they can learn it, and this is important in making decisions about selection, education, and placement. However, the IQ ideology goes considerably beyond these obvious facts and reinforces the image that people can be ranked for any given position from the worst to the best. Yet this image is highly questionable. Much like marriage, there is not just one Mr. or Ms. Right. There are often many—some, of course, never to be met (there are many Mr. and Ms. Wrongs, met and unmet, as well). And the "Right" ones are not all right for the same reasons and may not be rankable according to a set standard.

The underlying myth of studies like *The Bell Curve* is that people can be arranged in a precise hierarchy of ability, from lower to higher, and that in an efficient (and hence fair) allocation of positions the hierarchy of talent matches the hierarchy of positions. For each position there is one Mr. or Ms. Right. Once this myth is faced, as it must be by any society that is not to be locked into a nineteenth-century version of science, the arguments behind *The Bell Curve* fall apart. What those who want market efficiency should aim for is actually to maximize the number of people who are able to think and act together at high levels of proficiency and to do so in ways that provide added benefit to the society at large. While innate components should not be dismissed, intelligence should be treated as a product of social organization. Once the Mr./Ms. Right myth is rejected, then our way of thinking about the nature of intelligence and selection must change as well.

The point can be illustrated by the procedure used by one state-of-the-art Japanese automobile plant in selecting new workers. One of the tests involved a mock robot made of rods, nuts, and bolts. The human resource office would take a group of five candidates into a room with the robot. Also in the room was a pile of rods, nuts, and bolts, and the group was told that they are a team and their task is to make a robot out of the pile of metal parts. While some members of the team, often those with high mechanical ability or with military experience, would begin to tell the others what needed to be done, assigning each a different task or even taking on the job themselves, the scorers focused their attention on how well the individuals in the group cooperated with one another and created an environment in which everyone contributed ideas that would enable all to perform at a high level.

Of course the work required in an automobile plant cannot serve as a full model of intelligence (and market efficiency should certainly not serve as a complete and adequate goal for education), but it provides a good illustration of how an inadequate model of intelligence can be counterproductive and can contribute to the creation of inefficient performance. Like those participants who went about the task to demonstrate their own skills, and forgot the needs of the group, the testers focus on the individual level and neglect the need to enhance the performance of the collective. The great problem with research like *The Bell Curve* is that it diverts our attention from this level of the task.

AFFIRMATIVE ACTION AND POVERTY

There is one other objection to affirmative action that I want to begin to address in this chapter. This is the objection that affirmative action is an inadequate instrument to end poverty. Conservatives argue that it cannot help people in poverty because many lack the "threshold skills" needed for many entrance jobs (Eastland, 1996, p. 155). Yet many of these same conservatives also argue against government programs that would help people in poverty develop the threshold skills required, and perhaps more important, they fail to support social programs, especially free day care, that would provide parents the time to learn the skills or to take jobs that were available.

A strong case against this approach is made by the sociologist William J. Wilson (1987), who begins by summarizing many of the problems with the conservative belief that cutting welfare benefits to the poor will improve their chances of rising out of poverty. Referring to an earlier book by Murray, *Losing Ground* (1984), Wilson summarizes and supports the critics:

> For example, whereas Murray maintains that the availability of food stamps and increase in Aid for Dependent Children (AFDC) payments have had a negative effect on poor black family formation and work incentives, liberal critics have appropriately pointed out that the real value of these two combined programs increased only from 1960 to 1972; after that time, their real value declined sharply because states neglected to adjust AFDC benefit levels to inflation, yet "there were no reversals in the trends of either family composition or work effort." Moreover, in 1975, Congress enacted the Earned Income Tax Credit, which further expanded the advantages of working for the poor. Thus, if welfare incentives lead to black joblessness and family dissolution as Murray argues, "these trends should have reversed themselves in the 1970s when the relative advantage of work over welfare increased sharply." They did not, of course; black joblessness, female-headed families, and illegitimacy soared during the 1970s. (p. 17)

Yet Wilson (1987, 1996) too is concerned about the effects of programs like affirmative action and is concerned about the growing economic gap between lower- and higher-income Black people. He argues that while many of the race-targeted programs have aided the more advantaged of the Black population, they have done little to advance the situation of less-advantaged Blacks.

Although the increase in blue-color jobs for Blacks suggests that Wilson is underemphasizing the effect of affirmative action on poverty, he has sometimes been wrongly interpreted as supporting those who would abolish affirmative action. His point, however, is not that affirmative action should be abolished. As he puts it: "As long as minorities are underrepresented in higher-paying and desirable positions in society, affirmative action will be needed" (Wilson, 1996, p. 154). His point is that affirmative action should not be accepted as a substitute for broader economic policies that would create jobs. This is quite right. Affirmative action just assures that members of targeted groups are provided opportunities to be considered for whatever jobs are available—however many or few. It does not have as its primary goal the elimination of poverty, and as long as it is evaluated in those terms it will come up short.

Poverty should be minimized, and eliminated if possible, and the best way to do that is through programs that create jobs; that work with people in a way that provides the technical, social, and intellectual skills that are needed for good job performance; and that provide the health care, including drug counseling, and family services that are required in order to leave home and go to work.

Affirmative action is not necessarily a poverty remedy because it may have little to do with increasing the number of positions available. It accepts the existing number of jobs as a given and then seeks to widen the number and types of people who will be considered for them. The justification for doing this is that there is something wrong with the way the present deck is arranged and that some new arrangements must be considered.

Affirmative action is not a way to change the value of the entire deck, however. This is true even of need-based affirmative action (see Chapter 3), which would base affirmative action on economic need rather than race and gender. Unless there is some slack in the system, slack that allows one person to advance without another falling, this mode of selection will result only in people shifting positions. To do more—to address poverty— it is important to allow for such slack. Hence it is important not to confuse affirmative action with programs that might be more directly targeted to the poor. The other side of this is that it is important not to evaluate affirmative action as if it were an antipoverty program. It seeks fairness within a given distribution. It does not address the question whether the overall pattern of distribution is fair among economic classes. Even given the present conservative climate, affirmative action is not the only policy debate in town, and it should not be thought that by settling the questions it raises, all questions about educational and vocational justice have been resolved.

CHAPTER 3

A Case for a Backward-looking Gender- and Race-based Policy

I begin this chapter by examining an alternative approach to affirmative action, one that rejects on moral grounds the present emphasis on race and gender and pursues a need-based policy that would provide opportunities on the basis of social class, with poorer people receiving preference over wealthier ones. I argue that this substitute is inadequate because it does not address the moral concerns that a race- and gender-based policy does. I examine the moral foundations of the present practice and argue that a race-and-gender approach to affirmative action is not only morally defensible, but that it serves important ends that a need-based substitute does not. I show that many of the most important reasons for the present policy have been lost in an overemphasis on the role of affirmative action as a weapon against poverty, and in this and the next chapter I examine some of these other reasons.

In making this argument I am not rejecting the idea that need and social class have a role to play in determining the distribution of educational and occupational benefits, and in Chapter 5 I address this role. However, I argue here that need does not address a number of the moral reasons for the present policy. The argument presented here should not be taken to suggest that the present policy does all that is morally required; it just does some of those things.

THE PROBLEM: RACE-BASED OR NEED-BASED AFFIRMATIVE ACTION?

The recent criticism of affirmative action is related to political shifts in this country that have been a response to a changing sense of moral obligations and to the belief held by some that the liberal agenda has moved beyond a fair and just distribution of educational and occupational opportunities. Because affirmative action was enacted to aid members of specific groups to advance both in school and at work, critics argue it unfairly provides favorable treatment to members of some groups at the expense of others.

The most persuasive of the present critics are not those who would dismiss affirmative action entirely but those who would shift its target group from people of color and women to poor people of all kinds, including White men. These critics argue that affirmative action has strayed from the initial goal of the Civil Rights Movement, which they see as the restoration of equal opportunity that has resulted from generations of poverty and discrimination. This goal is violated, they argue, not only when White men are favored over women and minorities, but when women, Blacks, or members of other targeted minorities are selected regardless of their need or social class background.

One critic, Richard D. Kahlenberg (1996), points out that both Martin Luther King and Robert Kennedy became convinced shortly before they were assassinated that class and poverty were the principle lenses through which social inequality should be viewed. As Kennedy noted in an interview, "it was pointless to talk about the real problem in America being Black and White, it was really rich and poor, which was a much more complex subject" (p. xv) and King, shortly before his death, declared:

> We are going to take this movement and we are going to reach out to the poor people in all directions in this country. . . . And we're going to bring them together and enlarge this campaign into something bigger than just a civil rights movement for Negroes. (p. xiii)

The liberal critics of race- and gender-based affirmative action hold that it violates the King–Kennedy spirit and advocate instead class-based preferences, that is, preferences based on economic need.

Kahlenberg (1996) observes that the present policy is based on a slippage in reasoning. We have moved from the idea that because "poor kids have unequal opportunities and, because of past discrimination, an extraordinary number of poor kids are black" and should be given an extra break to the notion that "*every* individual black needs a break against *every* individual White, no matter the class status of each" (p. 17, emphasis in original).

There are obviously political as well as moral reasons to consider Kahlenberg's proposal seriously. Given the recent backtracking on affirmative action decisions, both in the courts and in legislatures, and given the growing sense that the moral foundation for the present practice is shaky, need-based affirmative action appears to be an attractive compromise. True, need-based affirmative action policies would no longer target minorities and women exclusively, but would instead extend the benefits of affirmative action to all talented poor people, including White males. As a result, affirmative action would become class- rather than race- or gender-sensitive. Yet many people of color, both men and women, and an increasing number of White women are poor, and would thus still be eligible for special consideration under a need-based approach. However, while many would still remain eligible, the estimate is that the number of Blacks actually selected would be reduced significantly.

Besides its anticipated political appeal, the moral attractiveness of the need-based alternative is that it fits many people's initial idea of fairness—that individuals should be given equal opportunity to advance independently of the deficits or benefits provided by their parents and without consideration given to "accidental" characteristics, like race and gender, over which they have no control. Indeed the appeal is across the political spectrum. Many conservatives view the alternative as a way to aid the "deserving" poor while some on the Left are attracted to the idea because they believe, with Kahlenberg, that class issues are more fundamental than those of race or gender.

CONSERVATIVE AND LIBERAL VARIETIES OF NEED-BASED AFFIRMATIVE ACTION

The need-based alternative to current affirmative action practices would change the focus of the program from one that seeks to open opportunities for women and members of certain minority groups to one that seeks to advance talented and motivated people from any group who may be held back because they are poor. This change has received support from both liberal and conservative camps. Both object to certain aspects of the present system, such as the possibility of granting preferences to children from professional families just because they happen to possess a Hispanic surname while providing no such preferences to talented White children from poor families. Many liberals and conservatives alike see this as unfair, and to the extent that choices of this kind are encouraged—as they are, for example, when Hispanic surnames are simply counted as meeting affirmative action standards—it appears as if affirmative action policy may serve to advantage advantage and disadvantage disadvantage.

Insofar as economic conservatives—those whose identity is defined by commitment to free market practices—can allow for government intervention, the need-based approach is consistent with their basic ideology of promoting market efficiency. It allows the difference in educational attainment and income to remain as it is, while enabling ambitious and talented people from all groups to rise to the top. It also assures that deserving individuals are not passed over simply because they are not members of some preferred group. Liberals and conservatives differ, however, in terms of the extent to which they want to define economic need in ways that would protect some of the gains made by women and minorities.

As we saw in Chapter 2, conservatives are generally not concerned about an unequal distribution of income, position, or status. The indifference is consistent with the general reluctance of the economic conservative to advance government regulation over private industry. Many conservatives believe that market factors alone are sufficient to correct for inadequate selection and that companies that overlook talented women or racial minorities will, in the long run, suffer competitive disadvantage and will lose out to companies that hire from the entire pool of talent regardless of race and gender. However, some conservatives allow that distortions may arise because of unequal educational opportunities, but they are, as reported by Hacker (1995), unconvinced that these distortions have any connection to race, and are therefore indifferent to the effect that a need-based approach would have on racial allocations (D'Souza, 1995).

In the case of gender inequality, this indifference is also consistent with the cultural conservative's commitment to the ideal of the "traditional" two-parent family with the mother at home raising the children and the father working outside the home to support them. Given these two commitments—the one to an ideal market, the other to an ideal family—inequalities are seen as acceptable differences within the market or as reasonable pressure to return to the norm of the "traditional" family.

Liberal supporters of need-based affirmative action differ from conservatives in their sensitivity to the race issue. They are concerned about studies that show that the actual consequences of need-based policies would be especially severe on African Americans and would result in a significant decrease in the number admitted to colleges and universities.

The Scholastic Assessment Test . . . still provides a rough measure of academic preparation. In 1993 approximately 14 percent of the 1,044,465 high school seniors who took the test came from families having incomes below $20,000. Among the white students in this presumably disadvantaged group, the average score was 872 out of a possible 1,600, while the Hispanic students averaged 725 and the black figure was 693. (Hacker, 1995, p. 38)

The results of a change from a race- to a need-based policy would clearly be to redirect some of the present-day resources that are being spent on certain minorities to White males. Of course, given the larger percentages of poor people among the ranks of presently targeted groups, it is reasonable to expect that White males would still have a comparably smaller percentage of their numbers receiving benefits. Nevertheless, given the size of the group, it is certain that a significant portion of present benefits would be shifted away from those who presently are eligible to receive them. Moreover, the shift from a race- to a need-based policy would have a multiplying effect. It would reduce not only the number of African Americans and other minorities admitted to competitive undergraduate colleges, but it would also reduce even more the number of successful applicants to graduate and professional schools.

In professional school, for example, not only would one have to subtract from the pool those African-American students who would lose seats because of the turn from race to need, but one would also have to subtract those who, having completed undergraduate college, would not compete successfully for professional places under less flexible guidelines.

This is illustrated by the admissions policies of the University of Texas that came under scrutiny in *Hopwood* v. *Texas* (1996). In order to correct the lingering effects of past discrimination, the University of Texas Law School decided to admit African and Mexican Americans in proportion to their graduation rates from Texas colleges—approximately 10% Mexican-American and 5% Black. To achieve this goal, however, the law school has adjusted its standards significantly and without racial preferences the university lawyers argue that few members of the targeted groups would have been successful. Although an admissions policy that reached further into the White working class, as need-based preferences would presumably do, would probably reveal many more Whites with lower scores, it would also dilute the number of successful applicants from some of the now targeted groups. Just how much dilution would occur at this second phase is difficult to say, since the change in policy would limit spaces in undergraduate school to Blacks who are more competitive. The same is true of President Clinton's favored rationale for affirmative action—that we must make a special effort to identify candidates who could make a distinguished contribution to the country.

Thus one of the differences between the conservative and the liberal approaches to need-based affirmative action is that the liberal does worry about its implications for racial distribution. Some liberals argue that any reasonably sensitive indicator of a student's level of disadvantage would yield a higher relative proportion of Blacks. Kahlenberg (1995), for example, advances a complicated rating scheme that would advance college applicants partly on the basis of a score on a disability index that would include parental income, education, and occupation as well as the quality of the applicant's secondary education, neighborhood, and family structure. The more disadvantaged an applicant is in these areas, the more points would be granted as a way to offset lower scores on admissions tests.

Such a system is proposed as a way to offset unfair disadvantages. Kahlenberg (1996) argues that this scheme would probably not result in significantly fewer African Americans being chosen for positions even given findings that suggest otherwise. The implication that we are supposed to draw is that under this scheme African Americans would not lose out in terms of numbers admitted, and that handicaps provided for disadvantages would actually result in a higher level of talent being represented in our nation's colleges and universities.

Whether this prediction would prove accurate is difficult to say. However, given the premise of the need-based alternative, one must wonder why liberals would still be concerned with the effects of such a policy on Blacks or any other group. If the problem is the underrepresentation of the *disadvantaged as such*, rather than the *Black* or *female* disadvantaged, why worry about a particular group of disadvantaged people? It would seem that we really should be concerned only about whether talented and motivated but disadvantaged applicants are receiving a fair shot at admissions and not whether successful applicants are Black, White, women, men, short, fat, thin, or tall.

Given the basic premise of the argument—that the problem is the disadvantaged as such—the conservatives have the day. Even test bias is not to be judged on the basis of whether some racial groups score at the same proportions as the majority. If our concern is the disadvantaged as such, and if we believe that the present college curriculum and grading policy are appropriate and impartial—issues the liberal proposals have not contested—then a test is biased only if it incorrectly predicts ultimate performance.

Kahlenberg and other liberals who seek class-based affirmative action are hedging their bets—a shift from race to class will not, they argue, really disadvantage race. But why would they hedge unless they thought that race presents—as I believe it does—a very special kind of disadvantage? Without such an assumption, the conservative critic could effectively point out that the liberal advocates of class-based affirmative action have decided beforehand which groups should be represented at the higher level and that, given this decision, they are simply trying to make it more acceptable to the White male population. Yet, the conservative might continue, if the aim is fairness and if we are truly open to the question of the cause of disadvantage, then why worry beforehand about whether a certain racial distribution results? Liberals who see merit in switching from a race- to a class-based form of affirmative action have yet to address this question.

SOME DIFFERENCES BETWEEN THE TWO APPROACHES TO AFFIRMATIVE ACTION

A need-based policy would shift the focus of attention away from group membership and place it instead on individuals and their economic situation. Advocates see the proposed change as forward-looking and future-directed. It rewards talented members of any group who are motivated to succeed and is thus a good social investment. A need-based policy is not only, they believe, consistent with many people's idea of fairness; it is also consistent with their idea of democracy because it serves to advance talented individuals regardless of their gender or race or religious background. A need-based policy would focus on the economic situation and would work to advance talented but poor students who would be otherwise overlooked.

Because this policy would be race-neutral, it is claimed that it would not stir up the antagonisms—at least among White men—that affirmative action does and yet because so many of the poor come from racial minorities that have been discriminated against, it would still tend to favor, although not in the same numbers, Blacks, Hispanics, and other disadvantaged groups.

The purpose of race- and gender-based affirmative action is different. It is to advance equal opportunity but to do so by reducing discrimination and increasing the number of minorities and women in the relevant positions. While there is obviously some overlap between economic status and group membership, the spotlight of affirmative action has not been aimed at the poor as such but at women and members of certain minority groups, some but not all of whom are also poor. The reasons for this are complicated and constitute much of the subject matter of this chapter. However, the general idea is that past and present discrimination has been systematically exercised against members of these groups and has thus resulted in the unjust suppression of talent. Many also believe that this discrimination is a violation of the constitutional right to equal protection. Advocates of the present practices believe that people from these groups historically have been *denied* the opportunities to develop their talent and to be admitted and hired on the basis of a fair competition.

Thus race- and gender-based affirmative action is justified on the grounds, not just that it seeks to correct *any* distortion in equal opportunity, but that it seeks to end the effects of past and continuing discrimination.

The present practice cuts across economic groups and holds that the effects of past acts of discrimination linger in the present for members of specific groups and that members of these targeted groups, no matter their present economic position, continue to be denied reasonable benefits and social standing. Past discrimination has, under this interpretation, handicapped all members of the targeted groups—even some who may be relatively well off economically. Affirmative action seeks to remove impediments caused by such discrimination and to enable members of these groups to advance as they would have done otherwise. In part the two approaches differ about the nature of these impediments.

It is true that the most publicized purpose of affirmative action is to reestablish the elements of fair competition that are embedded in the ideal of equality of opportunity and this is why a need-based approach seems consistent with the basic idea of affirmative action. Yet affirmative action as it presently stands aims to correct only certain kinds of distortions in equal opportunity—those that result from a history involving group stigma and that continue to have a present discriminatory impact. Because historical discrimination and its lingering effects apply only to members of some groups and not to others, the application of the principle of equality of opportunity should be circumscribed by affirmative action to members of these groups even though *individuals* from outside of these groups may have been the subjects of unfair treatment, bad luck, or other factors that may impact on economic well-being.

Those outside the targeted groups may appeal to equal opportunity to justify individual claims to advancement and may even successfully sue to counter individual acts of discrimination that blatantly favor individual women or minority members over a more qualified White man. And they may by accident or design fall within a policy intended to benefit targeted groups, as, for example, when it is required that certain positions be advertised widely. Nevertheless, the focus of affirmative action policy largely and properly remains women, the disabled, and people of color, who continue to experience the effects of systematic discrimination and group stigmatization. The purpose of targeting members of these groups is to remove a stigma that all members of the group have been marked with and that serves to assign individuals from these groups to positions of reduced prominence and opportunity.

Thus affirmative action differs from most other policies that are concerned to advance the ideal of equality of opportunity and that have focused attention on the impediments to advancement that arise because of economic need alone. This focus has been broadened in recent years by the emphasis on diversity that was mentioned in Chapter 2. However, this emphasis, as the basis for a legal policy, remains problematic both for the reasons given there and for others that will be developed later.

Because affirmative action is intended to correct for systematic discrimination among members of certain historically disadvantaged groups, it has not been, except in a limited sense, a need-based policy. For example, in theory at least, the critical spotlight of affirmative action might well shine on a college that eliminates women's gymnastics even though every member of the team comes from professional and upper-middle-class homes. In contrast, it might allow a college to eliminate men's baseball even though all the members of the team come from a White lower-working-class background. However, since most men's sports are well entrenched in colleges and universities, while women's sports are not, such cases are quite rare. And since the social-class composition, as opposed to the sex, of a team is accidental, the actual elimination of the baseball team would not be a case of class discrimination.

Need does come into play in an indirect way in the present policy given that the groups that have been the focus of affirmative action contain many of society's most economically vulnerable individuals. Yet when affirmative action is applied to them it is not just because they are economically vulnerable, but because of the effects of historical or systematic acts of discrimination. While there is a larger principle of equality of opportunity that lies behind the practice of affirmative action, it is the fact that this principle has been systematically violated for members of certain groups that motivates the narrower focus. It is in this sense that the present application of affirmative action is race- and gender- rather than need-based.

The need-based alternative presupposes that the only legitimate function of affirmative action is to correct inequities in the marketplace that arise because some talented women and some talented men from many different racial and ethnic groups are not well positioned to take advantage of educational opportunities and develop their talents. Those who advance a need-based view believe that every legitimate goal that is presently served by the race- and gender-based approach also can be served by the need-based approach—talented but poor and underachieving women and minority members will be identified and educated. However, they also believe that it will do more because it will also advance poor and talented White men. Yet this approach overstates the case in a number of important ways and misses some of the noneconomic factors that affirmative action, as it is presently practiced, is intended to meet.

First, the belief that affirmative action is primarily a way to smooth over any wrinkle in equal opportunity and improve the benefits of education to society at large is problematic. That a child of a single, alcoholic, destitute, slum-dwelling parent, with moderate test scores, has overcome more barriers and may therefore be as intelligent as the higher-scoring child of a Harvard-educated investment banker and Yale-educated lawyer is certainly plausible.

Yet there is something highly conjectural about the conclusion that the child of the single, alcoholic, slum-dwelling parent will contribute more to society than the child of the banker and lawyer. This is plausible only if one assumes that the support and cultural capital provided by family, friends, neighborhood, and so forth, will not continue to contribute to performance both in and after college. Yet the opposite seems more likely—the student who does not have to battle family and neighborhood influences while in college, and who can depend upon their emotional, psychological, and financial support, probably has the better chance of succeeding and making a greater social contribution, at least in the conventional sense. It may be the case that the pauper and the prince were switched at birth, yet the prince has spent years learning to be a prince and the pauper spent those same years learning to be a pauper, and it is hard to believe that those years would not count for something. True, it is important for society to continue to renew its talent base by continuing to reach into the ranks of the otherwise excluded to find and support those who can "rise above their circumstances" and compete with "the best" of them. Yet this does not require that added points be provided for those circumstances unless more is at stake than a wager over whether the advantaged or the disadvantaged student will produce greater benefits for society at large.

Conservatives may find the above argument to their liking, but they should not. It only highlights the obvious fact that family and community influence continue after students have left home and entered college and that any argument based on the mystery of hidden talents alone, talents that can only be read from a "what if" script, is on weak grounds. A student might well have hidden talents, but the marginal position of her family may require that more attention and therefore more resources be spent on her if her contribution is to be equal to that of some less talented but more secure student with higher grades and higher test scores.

Liberals may find the argument hard to accept, believing that it undercuts any efforts to address the situation of the poor. Yet the lesson here is not that we should ignore the situation of the poor. It is that we should address it directly as it exists in housing and joblessness and education at all levels and not use affirmative action as an excuse to do what should be done without an excuse.

The argument only undercuts the major rationale for need-based affirmative action. Without a stronger guarantee that society will benefit from such a policy, it is hard to see what would justify a government from reaching into the admissions policies of universities and requiring that they devise a formula that gives special privilege to the economically needy. One hopes that universities will do all that they can to support the talented needy once they are identified, and that society at large will support a public education system that assures a reasonable chance to all. A nation's interest in fairness and in renewing its talent pool would encourage such policy through special government grants and scholarships. To do less is to send a message that effort and talent do not count. Yet to *require* that programs admit students on the basis of need—as opposed to supporting them once admitted—is hard to justify given prevailing and reasonable assumptions about the right to self-governance of educational institutions. In contrast, for the government to fail to enforce race- and gender-based affirmative action is unjust.

The difference lies in the way the distortion of equal opportunity should be understood in cases of need on the one hand and cases of race and gender on the other. Under the need-based alternative, the assumption is that the student has been inhibited from expressing her true talent. The argument then holds that regardless of the cause of this inhibition, such students should be advanced over those who have achieved more but who have been inhibited less. Under this alternative, whether there is a history of discrimination against the child's group is irrelevant. The treatment is to be the same whether the child's parents have fallen into hard times because of discrimination or just because of bad luck or poor choices. True, the child's parents may have been discriminated against and as a result they fell into hard times, but then again they may have just fallen into hard times.

The idea that education should help all students achieve their potential is an educational imperative. This may entail aiding less fortunate students through additional tutoring in high schools, more funding for neighborhood programs, better family counseling, a jobs program, and encouraging some service and professional people to live in the neighborhoods where they work. Yet the simple fact that a student comes from a supportive home environment is not a good reason for requiring that a student with poorer grades and test scores be advanced into his place in the admissions line.

Universities may want to widen what they take to be "a better record," allowing that extracurricular or even work experience count as well as grades and test scores. However, any change along these lines may not necessarily favor the economically needy student, and surely should be decided by the individual institutions.

THE PRELIMINARY CASE FOR RACE- AND GENDER-BASED AFFIRMATIVE ACTION

The case for race- and gender-based affirmative action is different. In these instances too there is an assumption that talent has been inhibited. However, there is also the knowledge that there is an agent that has done the inhibiting and that, in many instances, continues to do so. More than misfortune is present here. Injustice exists as well. Given this difference, there are at least three reasons for supporting race- and gender-based affirmative action.

Economics versus Culture

Arguments for need-based affirmative action largely focus their critical attention on race and are mostly silent about women. To see the implications of this is to reveal an important weakness in the need-based alternative. Although raised in the same families as their brothers, and sharing largely the same economic benefits or deprivations, women have been systematically relegated to positions with less status and authority. This suggests that economic disadvantage is not the only roadblock to achievement. The reduced level of opportunity for women has been grounded in cultural and educational factors as much as in material ones.

In contrast, the need-based argument assumes that economic deprivation is primary and that it leads to cultural and educational deprivation. In fact, these three elements reinforce each other in the sense that what may begin as a cultural difference results in an educational difference that results in an economic inequality that in turn reinforces the cultural and educational inequality. If women are expected to work in the home, education need not be a high priority, and without a strong education, women have little choice but to work in the home.

It is certainly possible for one to accept the view that the primary goal of affirmative action is to correct inefficiencies in the market that result from misplacement of talented people without accepting the belief that the only cause of undeveloped talent is an economic one. This insight has been one of the starting points of a race- and gender-based approach to affirmative action, and it is largely overlooked by the need-based alternative.

Merit versus Standing

Another difference between the two approaches is that while both stress the importance of individual merit, the present practice seeks, in addition, to effect a cultural and psychological change that goes well beyond the benefits awarded to the successful individual applicants. Hence attention is focused on those who share certain "innate" characteristics—color or sex—and who, because of these characteristics, have been assigned reduced social standing. Because this reduced standing has negatively affected the aspirations of many and has frequently defined "normal" institutional practice, a systematic effort is needed to effect the desired change. Targeted assignment and selection is a way to educate the larger public about what *should* count as standing and to help all members of the stigmatized groups think differently about themselves.

Unlike a need-based approach, which functions to eliminate the one characteristic that is shared by all of those who are selected—poverty—and to separate those chosen from those not chosen, a race-and-gender approach selects people on the basis of features that will persist even after a change in educational and economic status has occurred. The change in status serves as a reminder that such characteristics should not be taken as a sign of reduced ability or competence.

Forward- versus Backward-looking Perspectives

Finally, those who argue for a need-based policy of affirmative action do so from what they see as a forward-looking perspective. Their goal is to advance the idea of equal opportunity and reduce inefficiencies in the economic system by assuring that talented applicants are not overlooked because of their economic situation. Certainly the present practice also advances forward-looking consequences, since any policy that finds and cultivates talent will increase the chances that society as a whole will also benefit. However, the present policy largely, although not exclusively, focuses attention on members of certain groups on the grounds that it has a special obligation to members of these groups as a result of past acts of discrimination. It is concerned to advance equal opportunity by aiding the search for talented individuals among those who, because of certain attributes such as race or gender, have been systematically excluded from certain positions. Thus whereas a need-based program is driven primarily by a vision of the future economic benefits to the society, a race- and gender-based program is driven to a large extent by the past treatment of certain groups and by the way such treatment impacts their present situation. Insofar as the effects are forward-seeking, they are so within a framework that brings specific groups into relief.

For example, to the advocates of a race- and gender-based approach, it will not do simply to toss a coin to determine the educational benefits of two equally talented, equally poor students when one belongs to a group with a long history of discrimination and the other is, say, a child of recent immigrants. Indeed, equal talent may be an unnecessarily high standard in many cases where affirmative action is called for. This is because sometimes affirmative action may involve an obligation to a specific group of people, whereas the selection of the most talented person among any and all applicants is best understood as a future investment for society at large and may entail selection from a different group. The moral force of this difference is well understood and is expressed, for example, when veterans are given certain preferences in exchange for a service rendered to their country.

Affirmative action often involves a special obligation owed to individuals as a result of their membership in certain groups. In these cases, to the extent that it is an investment, it is so within the confines of specific aggrieved groups. Affirmative action should be forward-seeking in the sense that wherever a choice is available society should seek to pay its debt in a way that will advance a relevant social interest. However, it must be emphasized that society *should* seek to pay its debts. This means that to the extent that debt is involved, affirmative action must involve a group-specific policy. In these cases the first aim of affirmative action should not be to maximize interests in general, but to serve the specific interests of members of the aggrieved group.

SUMMARY

In summary, there are three primary reasons for a race- and gender-based approach to affirmative action that a need-based approach fails to address. The first is to correct inefficiencies in the system resulting from systematic discrimination. In this case the need-based approach wrongly assumes that economic barriers should be given exclusive consideration.

The second reason for the present practice involves the educational and motivational benefits that may be served by advancing members of previously excluded groups into positions of authority and power. In this case the need-based approach fails to address the issue of stigmatized groups.

The third reason involves the issue of a social debt and the presumption that society, in its treatment of certain people, has incurred unusual obligations. The need-based approach fails here because it views affirmative action only in terms of a social investment. That the need-based substitute does not address these reasons very well should be an important factor in weighing its merits and demerits. However, before deciding whether the present approach should be maintained, there are some specific objections to the race- and gender-based alternative that must be addressed.

CHAPTER 4

Group Rights and Historical Obligations

There are two additional arguments against existing affirmative action practices and in favor of shifting the spotlight from racial and gender categories to economic ones. The first argument is that the focus on race and gender is inconsistent with American tradition and leads to a misguided conception of rights as belonging to groups rather than individuals. It is feared that this conception encourages people to form exclusionary idenities and to take their identity exclusively from their ethnic or racial group. Thus, the argument holds that if carried to its logical conclusion, the focus on groups would ultimately serve to Balkanize the nation. The second argument is that affirmative action holds innocent people accountable for the history of racism. I take these arguments in order.

DEFINING GROUP RIGHTS

The most common objection to affirmative action is that it is inconsistent with an emphasis on individual merit and advances the idea that people have rights as members of groups rather than as individuals.

There are two ways to think about a group right—a strict way and a permissive way—and it is only the first that is necessarily objectionable. In the first and strict sense of the term, the concept of a group right is employed to advance or protect the position of a people who share a certain identity and the right is granted or denied to people because of that identity. Here rights are afforded to a group, and people exercise them as members of that group. Because the right is granted to the group as such and held by individuals only as long as they belong to that group, a group right often serves to increase the coherence of the group by serving as a constant reminder to its members that their identity and their well-being are bound to their role as members of that group (Kymlicka, 1995).

48

A system of group rights in this strict sense places a strong burden on members within the group as well as on members outside to act in ways that recognize the group's integrity. Indeed to leave the group may quite literally mean to lose one's identity, as is symbolized by the orthodox Jewish family that grieves for the child who marries outside of the religion as if it were grieving for a child who died.

In a system of group rights, selected privileges are given to individual members just because they belong to a certain group, and others are denied for the same reason. While members exercise privileges, it is the group itself that holds the right to recognition. Individuals are recognized in terms of their status as members of the group. Hence, for example, individual Jews in the Middle Ages, unlike Christians, sometimes had the right to lend money for interest unless they converted to Christianity, at which time they lost the right. They often did not have the right to hold public office while they were still Jews. However, this right might be gained by conversion to Christianity.

A strong notion of group rights—one that is backed by state power—can have a number of obnoxious features, in part because the group is given the legal authority to control individual behavior in areas such as marriage, worship, dress, and work. In liberal societies, state power cannot legally support anything like this level of group rights (Kymlicka, 1995), although individuals may not be forbidden from voluntarily joining groups that would seek to exercise such control over them.

The contrast between this strong system of group rights and the modern system is captured by Michael Walzer (1990) in his description of the debate in the French National Assembly in 1771 over the status of Jews. The issue was whether they were to remain classified as Jews or were to be considered French citizens. Prior to this debate, Jews had separate group status and were recognized not as individuals or as citizens, but as Jews. When a vote on this issue was called in the National Assembly, the argument for the disestablishment of the Jewish corporate existence was summed up by Clermont-Tonnerre, "One must refuse everything to the Jews as a nation, and give everything to the Jews as individuals. . . . It should be repugnant to have . . . a nation within a nation" (quoted in Walzer, 1990, p. 609). The vote to change the status of Jews was, of course, consonant with the rise of individualism during this period and the idea that each citizen was to count as one person rather than as one member. Hence, for purposes of state, Jews are no longer members of a separate group, with distinct privileges and obligations, but now exist as individual French citizens who may or may not choose to associate with other Jews.

No one, of course, believes that affirmative action approaches anything like the system of separate group status described above. However, this is often the specter that forms the background to concerns about the Balkanizing effects of race- and gender-based policy. The confusion between the kind of group status exemplified by the Jews in France prior to 1771 and the kind that is implied by affirmative action can be captured by distinguishing between a group right and a group-*based* right.

The latter results when some people are wrongly denied the treatment that should be afforded to individual rights-bearing citizens because of a characteristic that they all share. The characteristic may be blue eyes, black skin, small bones, or the physical apparatus needed to bear children. The people who have this characteristic may or may not share a lot of other things, and they may or may not care about each other's welfare and they may or may not think of themselves as sharing an identity. All of this is irrelevant to the claim that they are not being treated fairly.

While it is true that affirmative action exists in part to advance equality of opportunity for members of certain groups, it is wrong to think of it in its present form as a group right in the first sense of the term. It does not seek to advance the coherence or the status of one group *over* another—although it may use an existing sense of identification in terms of role models to enhance its effect—nor does it seek to provide recognition to members of one group *over* another. It does not *give* special group status. Rather it uses group membership to identify and correct past acts of injustice that have resulted in present educational, economic, and social inequalities.

What affirmative action does is to draw on the second and looser sense of group rights, what I term group-based rights, in which individuals have certain claims because they share certain characteristcs. They do not have claims as a class because they are members of a certain group that exhibits qualities of coherence, self-identity, shared understandings, and external recognition. Sharing these qualities is accidental to the strength of any claims they make, and not sharing them neither strengthens nor weakens their claims. They have claims because each has a characteristic that is relevant for the claim being made, not because they have a single collective identity. A close analogue is the claim that ex-smokers who have contracted cancer might have against tobacco companies. To establish such a claim is not to establish that smokers constitute a coherent group. It simply allows that they have all been damaged in a similar way.

WHY AFFIRMATIVE ACTION IS CONFUSED WITH A GROUP RIGHT: THE STRATEGY OF SIMULTANEITY

One reason affirmative action is sometimes mistaken for a group right is because of what may usefully be called a strategy of simultaneity. This strategy is intended to increase, without quotas, the percentage of a group's representation in a given field by addressing both educational and employment opportunities and individual motivation at the same time. The strategy views opportunities and motivation as mutually reinforcing, and is based on the belief that opportunities and motivation are linked. Increase opportunities and motivation will rise as people from targeted groups begin to understand that there are openings for them; raise motivation and more opportunities will become available as employers and clients see more and more competent candidates from the targeted group. It is a policy that is intended to advance individuals' chances for fair treatment given underrepresentation resulting from historical discrimination suffered because of shared characteristics such as sex or skin color.

Simultaneity indicates policies that seek to increase the number of targeted minorities both within and between different fields at approximately the same time. It aims to change the cultural practices and self-conceptions that encourage discrimination or enable it to continue. The fact that some affirmative action policies are intended to lift the status of members of a group simultaneously should not be mistaken for the promotion of a group right in the strong sense of the term. Simultaneity is a strategic move that is intended to have the effect of breaking institutional deadlock where the action of isolated decision-makers is unlikely to have the desired effect.

To see this point, consider the once-long absence of African-American quarterbacks in the professional football leagues. It is hardly plausible that Black players lacked the natural talent to play that position until a few years ago. It is more likely that the prejudice of players, coaches, and owners resulted in this exclusion. What is hard to understand is why the profit motive or the desire to win did not override this prejudice long ago, at least among the poorer and least able teams.

One possible explanation has do with what Carmichael and Hamilton (1967) call institutional racism. One can imagine a situation in which at every level even the most well-intended coach would think that preparing a talented Black child for quarterback would be a disservice because of the perception that the coaches at the next level would never put a Black athlete in that position when there are White boys who can play it. This kind of thinking has the consequence that even the most well intended coach at the next level of play (say, high school) would have a double reason not to play a Black at quarterback: first, because the coaches at the lower levels have not trained any talented Black players for him to work with, and second, because the coach at the next level (say, college) has never played a Black at quarterback. And of course this situation undoubtedly has an effect on the inclinations of the athlete as well, who "realistically" wants to be trained for a slot where he has a chance of playing. Finally, there is an added effect on fans who, seeing no Black quarterbacks in the professional leagues, have the perception reinforced that Blacks are not suited for leadership positions. Thus a culture is created and maintained whereby, even if no one ever wished to discriminate, discriminatory practices are created and maintained.

Simultaneity is a strategic way to break such cycles. It is intended both to affect the way in which members of targeted minorities think about their opportunities for a good life within established institutional structures and to change the way in which established institutional structures respond to minorities. For example, an otherwise bright girl may well decide not to pursue a career in medicine if she is unable to associate womanhood with a medical career because she is not exposed to female physicians. Similarly, even if the medical school faculties wanted to increase the number of women in medicine they would have difficulty doing so if girls and young women, seeing few women physicians, decide to pursue different courses of study.

Simultaneity seeks to break this impasse by working on both ends at the same time. In this case it seeks ways to admit more women applicants into medical schools and into prestigious internships, while also encouraging more girls to pursue a course of study that would lead to medical school. The increase in the numbers of female medical students and physicians over the last decade and a half is an indication that affirmative action can play a significant role in addressing historically generated inequalities.

Simultaneity says that certain kinds of roadblocks are deeply rooted in historical and cultural practices and that special attempts must be made to remove them. It is a way to break those instances of underrepresentation that are the result of systematic and enforced past discrimination that has resulted in present cultural formations that continue to discriminate and reinforce reduced social standing. The policy is best understood not as reverse discrimination, as some critics have labeled it, but as a way to address historical and systematic acts of discrimination that have resulted in a collective level of competitive disadvantage or constrained motivation.

DO GROUP-BASED RIGHTS VIOLATE
OTHER PEOPLE'S INDIVIDUAL RIGHTS?

One objection to the policy of simultaneity is that even granting that the policy does not function as a group right on the inside, it does so on the outside. In other words, although simultaneity does not necessarily serve to strengthen the coherence of targeted groups, it does serve to deny to those outside of the group certain benefits that, as individuals, are rightfully theirs. Hence, for example, the White male applicant to law school with good grades and strong test scores is turned down and a place is given to a Black applicant with lower scores.

This issue is addressed with some success by Ronald Dworkin (1977) in his consideration of the *Bakke* (*Regents* v. *Bakke*, 1978) case. Dworkin sums up his argument as follows:

> Affirmative action programs seem to encourage, for example, a popular misunderstanding which is that they assume that racial or ethnic groups are entitled to proportionate shares of opportunities, so that Italian or Polish ethnic minorities are, in theory, as entitled to their proportionate shares as Blacks or Chicanos or American Indians are entitled to the shares the present programs give them. That is a plain mistake: the programs are not based on the idea that those who are aided are entitled to aid, but only on the strategic hypothesis that helping them is now an effective way of attacking a national problem. (p. 12)

For Dworkin, race, ethnicity, or gender would be an acceptable factor to use in admission if doing so serves an important national goal and if the exclusion that results is not based, as it was with, say, quotas *against* Jews and Blacks, on the view that one race or group is inherently better than another. He notes, for example, that potential legal skill, as reflected in scores on a law school admissions test, is obviously an important consideration in making selections to law school since it is generally better for a country to have available the services of more rather than fewer competent lawyers. However, skin color may also be relevant under certain circumstances such as when there is an undersupply of adequately trained lawyers available to serve a given racial or ethnic group. For Dworkin, racial preferences in professional programs such as medicine and law rest on a perfectly reasonable prediction that by admitting and training more Black or Hispanic lawyers and doctors this problem of underrepresentation will be addressed.

One of the things that is important to notice about Dworkin's argument is that it directs extra resources to any group in which an undersupply of professional or other relevant talent or resources exist. The force of this argument is to show that test scores or other signs of ability do not, by themselves, entail a right to a position and it thus allows for flexible standards of admission and assignment. However, his argument needs refinement because it does not recognize the differential merits of the claims of equally needy groups.

One problem with Dworkin's argument is that it is indiscriminate with regard to what it counts as a national problem and therefore is too broad a justification for what he seeks to support. Suppose, for example, that a new immigrant group is, along with African Americans, also under-served with regard to its professional talent in comparison with some national standard and suppose that special admissions could solve the problem. Given Dworkin's argument, members of this group would have the same claim on affirmative action resources as would members of un-derrepresented African-American communities. And this would be true even if they came to this country precisely because the quality of medical and legal services here is better than that available to them in their home-land.

Even though there are very good humanitarian reasons for providing adequate medical care and equal opportunity to members of new immi-grant groups, the implication that they should have an equal claim with Blacks to affirmative action is wrong from a moral standpoint. The moral force of affirmative action for African Americans is not just that they are less well served by professional talent than other Americans, although this is a condition that we should worry about. Rather, the moral force behind affirmative action for African Americans is based to a very large degree on the historical reasons that led to their being underserved.

Dworkin (1977) is both right and wrong when he says that "the programs are not based on the idea that those who are aided are entitled to aid, but only on the strategic hypothesis that helping them is now an effective way of attacking a national problem" (p. 12). He is right in the sense that no one, even those students with the highest grades and scores, is entitled to become a doctor. One is entitled to a place in a medical school only if there is reason to believe that a publicly recognized need will be met. He is wrong if he also assumes that African Americans do not have a special claim on the health resources of this nation, a claim whose justification includes but goes beyond the medical needs of the group.

One final concern with Dworkin's argument has to do with a possible implication regarding the way in which individual members of different racial groups are to be assigned places in the medical system. While Dwor-kin is probably correct that educating more Black professionals will proba-bly result in some improvement in the professional talent available to inner-city areas, affirmative action is certainly not the most efficient way to serve this goal.

If the primary goal is to increase the professional talent available to Black people, then professional schools should give priority to applicants who agree to spend a reasonable number of years serving Black people. It is likely that such a policy would give an advantage to African-American applicants, but it would do so only if they had the desired motivation, not because they are Black and not because Blackness has resulted in discrimination and reduced standing. However, while there is every reason to be in favor of a policy that seeks to select people who will serve underrepresented areas, and it is good public policy to provide added support to those who agree to do so, it would be racist to expect that only those admitted under affirmative action should be obliged to serve these areas.

AFFIRMATIVE ACTION AS ADDRESSING HISTORICAL DEBT

The moral basis of affirmative action involves more than addressing patterns of systematic discrimination and reduced standing. For Native and African Americans it also involves historical acts of such egregious nature that special obligations have been created for the larger society. These obligations are often confused with the other reasons for affirmative action, but they are inadequately captured by the kinds of moral appeals that otherwise would be quite acceptable. For example, the frequently expressed concerns of liberal defenders of affirmative action "to create a work force that reflects society at large" is consistent with attempts to correct perceived distortions in the marketplace of talent but it does not signal the presence of a historical debt.

The same is true of President Clinton's often stated rationale that we must make a strong effort to look for qualified candidates whose contributions, without affirmative action, would otherwise be lost. This argument does not suggest that there may be very different reasons why the talents of different individuals remain hidden and that such reasons are relevant in considering how such hidden talent should be acknowledged and treated. Nor is the problem of a debt fully captured by a notion such as "silencing," if this is meant to suggest that the problem could be adequately addressed simply by opening up avenues of communication and by giving those who have not spoken a voice, or by simply including their meanings in the conversation.

In the cases that I am addressing the task is not only to correct distortions in equal opportunity and to enable otherwise silenced voices to be heard. It is also to pay a debt that is owed as a result of unprecedented violation of human rights and liberties. Were such a debt to be widely acknowledged, as I will argue it should be, it would be clear that the problem with affirmative action is not that it offers too much, but that by itself it offers too little. The conclusion is not to eliminate affirmative action, a move that would clearly reduce the percentage of college-educated people and professionals from historically aggrieved minorities, especially African Americans, but to augment it in ways that would systematically address concerns of health, safety, and general education.

I am aware that to view affirmative action with regard to certain groups as a part of a historical debt goes against the tide of most thinking on the matter and is in need of justification. However, the fact that affirmative action is not concerned about the underrepresentation of all groups in all areas—for example, the proportion of Polish or Irish American CEOs—suggests that there is a prima facia recognition that members of different groups are positioned differently with regard to claims for assistance. Moreover, it also indicates that this position is the result not just of economic factors, but of unique historical experiences that so violated the human spirit that they create an overwhelming national obligation, and that this obligation, while never fully payable, must be constantly acknowledged and addressed in both spiritual and material ways.

The problem is not with the implicit recognition of the underlying moral intuition—that a debt is involved. Rather it is in specifying to whom and why it is owed. Liberals wrongly believe that to acknowledge such a debt involves acceptance of a group right in the pernicious sense of the term. Conservatives rightly reject the idea that *present*-day Whites are guilty of a *historical* transgression, but then wrongly conclude that because historical guilt is absent, so too is a debt. Supreme Court Justice Scalia's position (Fiscus, 1992) on this matter is the most challenging and it will be helpful to begin with it.

The Controversy over the Debt

Judge Scalia, one of the strongest opponents of affirmative action on the Supreme Court, is also one of the few officials to view it correctly in terms of a debt owed to certain members of our society. His opposition arises because he believes that the advantages provided to individuals from targeted groups by affirmative action policies are most often wrought from members of other groups who have not participated in the initial injustice and who were often in almost as vulnerable a position as those who receive its benefits. Justice Scalia expressed this objection forcefully:

> My father came to this country when he was a teenager. Not only had he never profited from the sweat of any Black man's brow, I don't think he had ever seen a Black man. There are, of course, many white ethnic groups that came to this country in great numbers relatively late in its history—Italians, Jews, Poles—who not only took no part in, and derived no profit from, the major historical suppression of the currently acknowledged minority groups, but were, in fact, themselves the object of discrimination by the dominant Anglo-Saxon majority. To be sure, in relatively recent years some or all of these groups have been the beneficiaries of discrimination against Blacks, or have themselves practiced discrimination, but to compare their racial debt . . . with that of those who plied the slave trade, and who maintained a formal caste system for many years thereafter, is to confuse a mountain with a molehill. Yet curiously enough, we find that in the system of restorative justice established by the Wisdoms and the Powells and the Whites, it is precisely these groups that do most of the restoring. It is they who, to a disproportionate degree, are the competitors with the urban Blacks and Hispanics for jobs, housing, and education. (quoted in Fiscus, 1992, p. 12)

Scalia is concerned whether anyone can be legitimately expected to pay the debt, but he quite openly suggests that, if anyone can be found who should pay it, there is indeed a debt to be paid. One of the questions he raises—albeit implicitly—is why one might think that some groups that have been discriminated against (e.g., Blacks) are owed a debt where as others, also discriminated against, are not owed one (e.g., European immigrants).

The most important thing about the debt is that it results from a forced, involuntary act that brings about serious and long-standing intergenerational disadvantages. Both sides of this are important. Many immigrant people suffered serious disadvantages when they came to this country in relation to individuals from other groups who were already here. However, even though some immigrants were forced to leave their native countries, they were not as a group forced to come *here*, and many came because they believed that here they would be better off than they were in their home countries. Clearly, many were discriminated against once they arrived, as Justice Scalia rightly points out, and it is still important from the point of view of fairness and equal opportunity that these discriminations, to the extent that they exist today, be removed. Nevertheless, they alone are not sufficient to warrant a targeted policy of affirmative action to address them, and this is because of a second point.

The important point of comparison is not just that members of a group were discriminated against or even that in some individual cases the physical and emotional harm could have been initially equal between members of two different groups. Certainly the life of Boston Irish immigrants in the last century was often a life of everyday degradation and humiliation. Indeed the remnants of this discrimination remain in terms like "Paddy wagon." Some modern-day descendants of European immigrants may well feel like Scalia that the fact that both European immigrants and African Americans suffered discrimination creates an equivalency that therefore invalidates the special claims of the latter.

Scalia wrongly assumes that the proper point of comparison is the initial treatment between different groups in this country and that an equivalency is established by virtue of the fact that both groups suffered an initial period of discrimination (although it is hard to see how anything could be comparable to slavery in its physical and spiritual degradation). However, the point of comparison is incomplete.

For example, with the exception of African Americans, Asian Americans, and Native Americans, the discrimination against Irish immigrants may have been matched by that against few others in the last century (Ogbu, 1991). Yet affirmative action is not an appropriate policy for Irish Americans not just because they have now reached parity with other groups, but because, in addition to their voluntary immigration, their standing was still comparatively better here than it was in Ireland. It is not only the level of material degradation that affects the judgment about how well or poorly members of one group faired in comparison to members of another. It is also the conditions under which they arrived in this country to begin with. To arrive as an involuntary slave in shackles, with one's family and cultural ties destroyed, is an act of extreme physical and spiritual degradation that cannot be captured by the word *discrimination*.

Regardless of the issue of to whom the debt is owed, Scalia believes that its costs are an unfair burden on the nondiscriminating immigrants, and because of this he believes that affirmative action itself is unfair. It forces payment from those who were not victimizers. The assumption that Scalia makes is that those who did not benefit directly from the initial act of discrimination are not obliged to compensate for it. Yet his conception of benefits is overly narrow, myopically focused on the individual, and confuses guilt and obligation. Certainly he is correct to suggest that his father should not be thought guilty because of slavery. However, this is not the same as saying that no obligation is owed.

Scalia's argument takes no account of the national capital that accrued as a result of the *forced* backbreaking labor of slaves, nor does he consider how such labor contributed to the eagerness of immigrants to come here. Certainly he and his father benefited from this labor—without it America would have been an even harsher place for new immigrants—and the question is whether, because of this benefit, a debt is owed.

Suppose that instead of slavery being assigned to members of a specific racial group, it had been assigned on a random basis to all new immigrants. Suppose that potential immigrants knew, before leaving home, that they would be randomly assigned to positions in the new land and that many would be wrenched from their families, chained together and crammed into ocean ships where many would die, and where those who lived would arrive here as slaves with no control over the well-being of their children.

Suppose too that they knew that this number was considerable, comprising about 15% the overall American population and 50% of the overall population in the southern states. Given this random assignment it is hard to imagine that many European immigrants who chose voluntarily to come to America would still have taken the chance to do so—including Scalia's father.

This scenario, borrowed from John Rawls (1971) and then amended to fit slavery, does not lose its force as generations become more removed from slavery. Not only must the population of potential slaves be randomized, but also the arrival period of the various immigrant groups. Similarly, we must add into the equation the social, economic, and legal stigma that remains with one's children as a result of having slave ancestors.

This is one reason why Scalia's argument does not have the moral force that he believes it has. To the extent that slave labor was needed to support the real—not some ideal—economy of the United States, we all benefit. The descendants of volunatry immigrants benefited in two ways. First, their ancestors' exemption—the fact that they could be assured that they would not wind up as slaves—made immigration an acceptable alternative, the fruits of which the descendants would eventually come to share. Second, the descendants of immigrants benefited because they never had to carry the lower standing that being a descendant of a slave entailed.

Granted, Scalia's argument is only incidentally about benefits. It is first and foremost about obligations. Do those who benefited from an earlier act of discrimination, even if not the perpetrators of that discrimination, have an obligation to those who were its victims? The crucial issue is what if any obligation the children of immigrants have when they or their ancestors, who were once subject to discrimination, now stand as the beneficiaries of the forced subjugation of others. Scalia seems to believe that they have none. I believe that he is wrong.

Granted, under some conditions the person who benefits from an act of discrimination does not owe a debt to the person who is discriminated against. Consider this example: I have just been turned down as a renter for a house because unbeknownst to me the landlord is anti-Semitic. You then come along and rent the house that otherwise would have been rented to me. You do not know of my rejection and had nothing to with it. Clearly the landlord owes me some compensation if I can prove my case. However, your role is benign and you should not be the party providing me compensation. You are in a better position than you would have been had the discrimination not occurred, but this position does not make you liable.

However, the lack of an obligation to compensate in the above instance relates only to a legal context. To the extent that a landlord must pay for discrimination, and to the extent that the market will bear it, the cost of that payment will be passed on to renters. There are benefits to go with those who exist as nonvictims and nonperpetrators within a climate of discrimination, and there are certain costs involved to these same people when a price is paid by the perpetrator for past discrimination.

The moral obligation is considerably higher if you actually know about the initial discrimination and then act so as to take advantage of it. In such cases you are indeed liable for the benefits you receive at the expense of others. Moreover, you are liable even if you have also been the victim of discrimination or if your material condition is the same as, or even worse than, my material condition. This is obvious. One is not excused of an armed robbery, say, because one is on food stamps.

Scalia is also wrong in his view that the discriminated-against offspring of an immigrant did not discriminate against the child of the slave. The color of trade unions and neighborhoods tells a very different story. True, there are many reasons why this discrimination was the expedient (perhaps even necessary from an individual standpoint) thing to do, but it was still discrimination.

Immigrants understood quite well that they were connected to a stream of opportunities that could be cashed in by future generations of their children and that is precisely why many of them came to this country and endured the hardships involved in choosing to do so (Handlin, 1951). They were also aware that Blacks were not a part of this stream, and sadly many times they fought to keep it this way. This continued history of discrimination against the children of slaves adds to the debt in more than material ways.

In contrast to the benefits the immigrant could anticipate, at least over some generations, slaves were denied not only the right to earn and to vote, but also the right to have their intentions receive public standing, even when those intentions involved the disposal of the wealth they created. Moreover, their descendants had to continue to struggle for these basic emblems of public standing (Shklar, 1991). To be the descendant of a slave is still to be involved in a significantly reduced stream of intergenerational opportunities and benefits as well as a degradation of everyday life. The reduced quality of everyday life is reflected in greater difficulty in renting and buying a home, higher prices asked for automobiles, slower service in stores, greater surveillance on the street, more frequent rejection of qualified job applicants. When contrasted to members of other groups who belong to the same generation, African Americans continue to experience the effects of reduced opportunities.

There is something quite right about Scalia's concern that there is a problem when we attempt to address these injustices, but it is important to be clear about what the nature of that problem is. The problem is not that compensation is provided or that children of immigrants, even those who themselves have been victimized by discrimination, have an obligation to provide some of it. It is that the burden sometimes does falls unduly on the most disadvantaged of these groups, especially in the places where people of color have advanced, and that the burden is not adequately shared. It is also that the burden of repaying the debt falls unevenly on White males who are entering the labor market and that a large part of the remaining population—including older White males—remains largely untouched. Scalia's concern is best illustrated by the case in which, say, all of us benefit from a past injustice but one young White male blue-collar laborer is singled out to pay the cost.

Yet the courts have recognized this problem and have been reluctant to address past discrimination when the cost would fall unevenly on a single individual rather than on a more diverse and unspecified group. Thus, for example, the Court has been more friendly to encouraging preferential hiring where many are denied and but one is chosen than it has been to accepting preferential firing where specific and identified individuals bear the cost of correcting generalized past discrimination. One exception to this is where companies have begun to correct a history of past discrimination and where seniority policies would result in layoffs for minorities who were recently hired to correct this history.

However, the fact remains, as Scalia correctly reminds us, that there is a certain cost in affirmative action policy to some individuals even if the specific individual who is bearing that cost is not known. If race were not a consideration, there are indeed instances in which, on the basis of grades and test scores, some other student would have been admitted to medical school or some other applicant would have gotten the job even when we comfortably do not know who that might have been.

Yet race *is* a consideration partly because it has operated across generations to skew the present-day competition in a way that, without a vigorously enforced affirmative action policy, perpetuates a pattern of selection that has been directed against other individuals—in this case,

African Americans—by historical and persistent patterns of discrimination. Thus without affirmative action it could be said that some present student would have been denied admission to medical school or some successful applicant would have failed to be admitted to college. And this would have been the case even though these students stand as victims of a long string of historical discrimination that, if it had not have occurred, might have allowed them to compete successfully without special preference.

What Scalia's objection suggests in the case of African Americans is not that race-based preferences are unjust but that there is a need for the burden to be shared more widely. It is not an argument, as he seems to think, for rejecting the idea of affirmative action altogether, nor does it adequately support his insinuation that there is no burden at all because there is no one single person who actually owes the debt. To share this burden more widely should involve policies aimed at rectifying the full cultural, social, and economic damage that has arisen following the American holocaust that was slavery and the slave trade. There are many ways to do this, but a general surtax on incomes over a certain minimum aimed at creating more professional programs and general support services for African Americans and members of other groups that meet certain criteria would be a useful addition to existing policy and would distribute the burden more equitably.

TO WHOM IS THE DEBT OWED? A RETURN TO THE QUESTION OF GROUP RIGHTS

Yet if Scalia is wrong and we agree that a debt is owed, there is still an issue regarding to whom the debt is owed. It is not immediately obvious that the debt is owed to the descendants of the slaves, since it was not they but their slave ancestors who were the target of the harm and who suffered the actual harm of slavery. Indeed, one avid defender of affirmative action, Fiscus (1992), rejects the idea that we owe present-day African Americans anything because of the harm that was done to their slave ancestors, and he rejects this idea because he believes that it is a racist ground for offering the benefits of affirmative action. His argument is worth considering in detail because it will help us to clarify the nature of the debt owed.

Fiscus (1992) argues against a justification of affirmative action on compensatory grounds because

> to hold that descendants of the millions of blacks harmed throughout our
> history are entitled to compensation for the long-past injury of their ances-

tors is to violate the first principle of compensatory justice – that recipients of compensation be the ones harmed. (p. 10)

He rejects, as racist, an alternative idea that all Blacks are equivalent to members of one family and therefore deserving of compensation. This rejection is based on his belief that such a notion

> equates, legally and morally, individual black men and women with their racial identity. It says that race is more important than anything else in determining worth and responsibility – indeed, in determining basic identity. It is, in a word, racist. (p. 10)

Similarly racist to him is the idea that the present "generation of whites should pay for the sins of earlier generations" (p. 10).

Fiscus's (1992) alternative is to accept the assumption that talent is distributed equally among the races and, on the basis of this assumption, to view underrepresentation as a sign of injustice that must be corrected. The legal force of the argument then lies in the enforcement of the equal protection clause. "Distributive justice as a matter of equal protection requires that individuals be awarded the positions, advantages or benefits they would have been awarded under fair conditions" (p. 13). Under this view, whenever there are proportionately more Whites in a position than are represented in the larger society, we have a probable instance of discrimination even if Whites lay claim to those positions "using putatively more objective measures of merit" (p. 13).

Whatever we may think about the racial distribution of talent – and there is good reason to think as Fiscus does that African Americans are usually placed lower than Whites of equal innate ability (Feinberg, 1983) – this argument has many weaknesses. First, it fits any group that does not have its proportional share of positions and certainly serves to water down any special claim that Blacks might have. Second, even if one does assume an equality of talent, there are other nondiscriminatory factors that may play a role in the distribution of positions. Interests is one of these as is the cultural capital of the family in relation to positions within the larger society. A family of musicians is more likely to produce musicians, even given equal innate musical talent, than a family of non-musicians. To ignore these factors or to believe that they require state action to "correct" is to impose a standard of uniformity on cultures that would be intolerable for all.

Since Fiscus rejects the idea that we should compensate for past injustices, it is hard to see, even if the present differences arose as the result of past discrimination, why present individuals should be expected to pay the price. He rejects this idea as racist when it comes to compensatory justice, but it is hard to see why he should think it any less racist when applied to distributory justice. Unless he believes that there is some unfair historical basis for the way talent is presently expressed in grades and test scores, then surely it is racist to deny a position to a White person on the basis of some abstract assumption regarding equality.

Consider that Fiscus's argument begins at the point at which two individuals—one Black and one White—have decided to compete for a given position. Yet much of the problem of representation comes well before the decision to compete and arises at the level of interest, motivation, self-concept, and the like. The fact is that many individuals do not enter the competition because, for a variety of reasons, they have been persuaded to pursue other, less competitive avenues.

Any reasonable affirmative action policy would surely want to address the problem at the level of motivation and interest as well as at the level of native ability. Motivation and interest, however, connect to a history in which what any present-day student may want for herself is connected to what that student's parents and grandparents were *allowed* to want for themselves. Yet if we are barred from looking backward to find the reason for compensation, as Fiscus's argument suggests, then the fact that the difference between my present interest in law and your lack of interest in the same subject can be accounted for by the fact that racism barred your grandfather from pursuing a career that mine was encouraged to entertain should be irrelevant.

The priority that Fiscus's argument gives to talent across groups is indiscriminate in terms of cause and therefore provides too broad a criterion for the application of affirmative action principles. One need not believe that there must be an exact correlation between the distribution of talent and the distribution of positions in order to believe that a distribution is unjust. There are, as Dworkin (1977) correctly points out, many legitimate reasons for choosing one applicant over another, and some of these are not exclusively related to talent in the more obvious sense.

This is important to recognize for a number of reasons. One of these is that it blunts the relevance of research that reinforces racist assumptions and institutions (research that Fiscus's argument inadvertently encourages) by claiming to prove that the racial variation in IQ scores is due to genetic factors (Herrnstein & Murray, 1994). A second is that it casts doubt on the morally questionable assumption that professional education and status is a reward that one has for being born with high intelligence regardless of what one does with that status. One does not need to assume equality of talent in order to judge a distribution of positions unjust. All one needs to assume is that for most positions more than enough people possess an *adequate* amount of talent to do the job at a high level of competence, and that moral reasons for selecting some segment of the adequately talented are being systematically ignored.

Finally, one need not be as concerned as Fiscus is about the reportedly racist assumption behind the idea that African Americans belong to a single group and that it is because of harm to past members of the group that they are owed compensation. To argue that someone is owed compensation because he or she possesses a certain trait in common with others—even membership in the same family—is not to claim that individuals are to be identified with that trait and only with that trait in each and every respect.

Suppose, for example, that I am told that I am one of but five living relatives of a recently deceased and very wealthy person and that all five, none of whom even know each other, are entitled to a fifth of her estate. Given that none of us knew the other before this bittersweet news, there is little reason to think that we have much in common or that we need to be treated the same in any respect other than that involving the liquidation of the estate. True, we belong to the same family, but that is probably a very incidental part of who we are, even though in this instance it is the sole determinant of what we are owed.

Without the reference point of slavery it is hard to understand why we should pay more attention to the lingering causes of discrimination against Blacks than the lingering causes of discrimination against immigrants. True, the lingering effects of discrimination against African Americans persist more intensely than discrimination against voluntary immigrants, but it is not clear that this always holds with respect to discrimination against newer groups such as Koreans and Vietnamese, who often experience hostility from Whites and Blacks alike. Whatever the statistics of well-being between different groups may be, without the distinguishing experience of slavery, any difference is one of degree, not of kind.

Fiscus objects to rooting the consideration back to slavery because he believes that doing so is racist, and while he is wrong in this objection, it is important to see in what way he is wrong. Earlier I noted that the point of comparison for the immigrant is the difference between how life might have been there and how it actually is here. I then noted that for the present-day African American the parallel question might be how his or her condition might have been without the institution of slavery in comparison with what it actually is. For most immigrants the right answer is probably that life here is better in some important ways than it would have been there. Yet an astute critic could make a similar case for the great-grandchildren of slaves.

The critic could note that for any particular present-day African

American the right answer is not that her life would have been better without slavery. Rather, the right answer is that this particular life would not have been at all and this is because of the simple fact that the genetic materials that comprise her biological self would not have been and that the person that is thought of as *her* simply would not have existed (Jefferson McMahan, personal conversation, 1995; see also Sher, 1980).

Now this answer is problematic from a moral point of view only if one believes as I do that extra consideration is due to the descendant of the slave and that the slave's descendants have claims that the child of the immigrant does not have. It is problematic because it complicates the base of comparison and, given the assumption that living is better than not being born, suggests that slavery provides no harm—in a strict sense of that term—to the present-day descendants of slaves.

Given this response, the question remains why should one think, as I do, that given two children we owe more to the child whose great-great-grandparents were enslaved than we do to the one whose great-great-grandparents worked in a sweatshop and that we do so even if the material conditions of the two great-great-grandchildren are presently similar. After all, while not all of the wealth created by the latter was stolen, as it was in the case of the slave, a lot was exploited.

Up to now I have treated the comparison between the immigrant and the slave as unproblematic, leaving it to moral intuition alone to decide that something more is owed to those whose ancestors were forced to come here when compared with those who had a choice. Now I want to press those intuitions by asking: Why should the question of whether immigration was forced or voluntary matter to the grandchildren of the original sojourners? Indeed, if we say that the grandchild of one is better off here than she would have been if she stayed in her original country, should we not say of the grandchild of the slave that she too is at least not worse off because of slavery than she would have been without it? My point is not that she is better off here than she would have been if the family had been permitted to stay in Africa. To say this is to assume that without slavery everything would have remained the same—except better. Yet, as noted above, without slavery everything would have been different including those who are now alive. Hence, it could be argued that in both cases—that of the immigrant and that of the slave (Sher, 1980)—the original decision did not harm the descendants even though in one case the decision was a voluntary one and in the other it was made by others, first through kidnapping and second through enslavement. Granted the descendant of the slave is probably less well off than the descendant of the immigrant, but so too are the descendants of newer immigrants less well off than descendants of older and the descendants of some who remained in parts of Africa are less well off than the descendants of some who were forced to come here.

Certainly the fact that, say, the Polish American had an ancestor who *chose* to come to this country while the African American's ancestor was *coerced* into coming made a big difference to the ancestors themselves. However, why, one might ask, should it make a difference to their *descendants* if, in both cases, their descendants are better off than they would have been had the fate of their ancestors been different? True, the child of the Polish immigrant is better off than she would have been were it not for the institution of slavery, but then so too is the descendant of the slave. True too the descendants of Polish immigrants are better off, on average, than descendants of slaves, but this resurrects Fiscus's (1992) problematic assumptions. The answer requires that discrimination against African Americans be seen as different in kind—not just in duration or intensity—from discrimination against European immigrants.

A Debt Owed to the Slave

Fiscus (1992) is quite right—we do not owe a debt to *present* individuals as compensation *because* of the harm done to their ancestors by slavery. However, he is wrong to assume that no debt is owed to anyone. Rather the debt is owed to the slave and just as with a will the debt to the slave is not cancelled once the slave has died or once slavery has ended. Fiscus, of course, would object. If the debt is owed to the slave, what sense does it make to pay off the descendants of the slave? If I steal money from you, I have not paid my debt by compensating your brother or your neighbor. Why then should it be thought that I have paid it if I compensate your great-grandchild, or nephew, or your neighbor's great-great-nephew or grandchild?

There are two answers to this question. The first is that as with any debt where the line of beneficiaries has blurred, one does the best one can, and in this case it is obvious that the descendants of slaves in general is the best that one can do to compensate any particular slave. Yet this answer tells us why descendants of slaves deserve compensation. It does not, to return to a point made earlier, say why they deserve to be compensated in a way that the descendants of immigrant wage laborers do not. After all, it could be argued that while it is true that slaves had all the fruits of their labor confiscated by others, immigrant wage earners had a lot of their labor confiscated. Hence while they might not have labored for as long or had as much of their labor stolen as did the slave, nevertheless the same principle would hold.

The second answer to the question of why compensation is owed the descendant of the slave is that present-day descendants of slaves deserve compensation because the institution of slavery violated essential elements of collective and individual autonomy and that this institution and those that followed it must be seen as accountable for many of the problems confronting the African-American community today.

The situation with immigrants is very different. While immigrant labor was exploited, immigrants were still allowed the autonomy to form intentions and to act on them, including intentions to have families and the expectation that these families would remain intact even after a long voyage and separation. Moreover, immigrants' intentions were publicly acknowledged and the fruits of their labor that remained after death were disposed of as it was willed. True, where severe exploitation existed, immigrant wage earners were often allowed to pass on only a relatively small amount of what they might, under fairer circumstance, have had a right to pass on. Nevertheless, the right to have intentions recognized and to be acted on through publicly sanctioned practices and institutions formed a framework for cultural empowerment that was not available to slaves. What this means in simple terms is that immigrants, while denied one kind of opportunity, were positioned so that subsequent generations could take advantage of other kinds of opportunities that happened along and that this was not the case for the children and the grandchildren of slaves. Unlike the slave, the laborer never lost *the right* to pass on material wealth, although some lost a lot of the material wealth that might have been passed on. Nevertheless, a primary motivation allowed to the immigrant, but not allowed to the slave, was that of intergenerational advancement, and over time such advancement often did occur.

For the slave the situation was different. It was not first and foremost wealth that was stolen. Rather, the right to be considered as the kind of being who could possess wealth and meaning was denied. There was, of course, a theft of material wealth—of the wealth created by sweat and blood. However, this was only a secondary loss since slaves were not allowed to be thought of as property owners. The first loss was the loss of public recognition as full human beings—as beings capable of creating meaning and developing property—a loss that involved the public denial of intentionality and of their right to have rights. (This loss is intensified because it occurs in the context of a society in which everyone else is supposed to be equal.) And this loss—public denial by the dominant group—has cultural and intergenerational as well as individual significance, and continues to rupture social standing and well-being.

The loss is the rupture of a would-be string of meanings and intentions that, when reconstructed, extends from the initial victim to those individuals in the present generation who are the otherwise beneficiaries of would-be stolen labor—"would be" because the concept of theft, at least for the slave, did not apply in the legal sense and it is this that is the larger affront to morality than mere theft. The material wealth that was lost and the means for repayment is a stand-in, a token, for the spiritual theft that still cuts across generations. It is represented in a reduced status and in an attitude on the part of members of society, even many newer members, that material deprivation, as represented by lower levels of income, housing, education, and health, is a more natural, more acceptable, position for African Americans than it is for the rest of us. Affirmative action as it presently exists is, of course, an inadequate mechanism for correcting this loss. Its only advantage is that so far it is better than any other alternative that is yet on the table.

It is not only, or even primarily, the liberal principle of equality of opportunity that was violated by slavery. It is the conservative and even more primary principle of the right to hold property and the right to pass it on to whomever one wants, a right that requires the social recognition of one's intentions.

Yet the violation that was slavery goes deeper than the question of private property and its legitimacy. Married women were also denied the right to own property in certain periods, but they were not denied the right to pass on property to their *male* offspring, and they were not held as property to be bought and sold. What was therefore violated was not just this or that individual's rights, although this certainly is part of the violation. Nor was the violation just a violation of a specific right or set of rights—property, free speech. It was the right to be considered a person and to establish the prerequisites required to flourish across generations.

To see the violation in terms of intergenerational flourishing instead of just in terms of individuals does not necessarily imply that all present-day African Americans are somehow the same or that their identity is exhausted or even confined by their racial identity, as Fiscus (1992) fears it does. Nor does it imply that all African-American people are only and exclusively a part of one culture and that is African-American culture. Like everyone else, African Americans can belong to many different cultural groups and have many different beliefs. There is no essential paradigm to which all African Americans must conform. Yet it is not just as stand-ins for the object of the slaves' would-have-been-intentions that the claim for special consideration is made. The assault on a culture has real consequences for many people in terms of truncated expectations and opportunities both denied and overlooked and in terms of a general social attitude on the part of others that accepts as part of the natural state of affairs lower levels of material well-being.

Affirmative action—that is, race-based, backward-looking affirmative action—can be part of a strategy for repairing the rupture. It attempts to reconstruct the opportunities to which intentions and expectations must be attached. It is less than adequate because it involves relatively few positions assigned to a relatively few individuals, and cannot serve as a substitute for the material benefits enjoyed by the rest of us as a result of a history that included the institution of slavery. Yet it surely should have a place in a policy of reconstruction. For example, an important complement to affirmative action policies in higher education might include the establishment of extended funding programs for Blacks and other targeted groups, based on financial need. At a time when the main cause of declining Black enrollment in and graduation from higher education is economic, affirmative action policies that fail to consider financial factors are by themselves insufficient (Sudarkasa, 1988).

SUMMARY

Those who believe that existing race- and gender-based affirmative action policy should be replaced by need-based considerations assume that existing affirmative action policy violates the principles of fairness and equal opportunity by advancing people because of certain accidents of birth. The argument in this chapter has shown that there are strong reasons to question this interpretation of existing practice and to be skeptical of proposals to replace it with a need-based program.

However, to reject the idea that a blanket consideration of need can serve as a substitute for considerations of race and gender should not be taken as an argument that need is irrelevant and should have no place at all in considerations of merit. Need has a role to play, but it is not a solo one. For example, structural changes that have taken place over the better part of this century have served to reduce the opportunities for intergenerational mobility for the children of unskilled and semi-skilled laborers, many of whom are recent immigrants. These structural changes, if not addressed, may well serve to create many of the same conditions that the present affirmative action policy has been designed to address, such as the mobility deadlock caused by the way in which lack of educational and economic opportunities reinforces certain social definitions and cultural practices that then serve to constrain motivation and opportunities, which in turn reduce educational and economic opportunities. Unlike in the case of African Americans, there may not always be a strong argument that a historical debt is owed here, and unlike women, members of these groups may not be spread among the different economic classes. However, to the extent that mobility for members of all groups is important, need is important. It is not a substitute for race and gender, but it still has a role to play. The concluding chapter addresses this role, and it also reexamines the place of diversity in affirmative action.

CHAPTER 5

Need, Diversity, and Group Variation

In this final chapter I address two concerns. First I return to the idea that affirmative action should focus on economic need and cultural diversity, an idea I dismissed earlier as the primary reason for affirmative action. Here I argue that even though these concerns should not serve as the primary basis for affirmative action, they should have a role to play in affirmative action programs that target racial and gender inequality.

Second I show how the three principles that I advanced as the primary reasons for race- and gender-based affirmative action apply to different claims. I show that in applying the principles, various considerations will weigh differently depending on the character of the group itself, its history, and its relation to the larger society. The presence of injustice is different for people from different groups, and, depending on the nature of the group and the injustice, the reasons for affirmative action will vary.

A REVIEW OF THE ARGUMENT

I have defended race- and gender-based affirmative action against attempts to eliminate it entirely or to replace it with programs that target social class and economic need. The central argument has been that race- and gender-based affirmative action serves sound moral and strategic concerns that critics of affirmative action have failed to address. I have also shown why, for some groups, the present policy, while morally necessary, is not sufficient. Hence in contrast to many present-day critics who believe that affirmative action provides too much, I have shown that, for some, it provides too little.

To review: race- and gender-based affirmative action seeks

1. To correct systematic ruptures in the exercise of the principle of equal opportunity
2. To advance the standing of groups whose members have been dis-

criminated against because of certain ascribed characteristics such as gender or skin color
3.   To redress cases of historical injustice

These three goals have a special moral force. They connect important social principles, both conservative and liberal. These goals emphasize the conservative idea that people are bound together into a social order only when they can count on others to acknowledge and pay their debts and that society must acknowledge and honor people's wishes regarding the transfer of property after their death (Nozick, 1974). They also connect to the liberal idea that people must be judged on the basis of relevant criteria when it comes to educational and employment opportunities, and that where inequities have developed and continue because of a group stigma, steps must be taken to remove the stigma from individual members of the group.

RETURNING TO THE ROLE OF NEED
AND DIVERSITY

In this defense I have mentioned and tentatively put aside two alternative justifications for affirmative action, arguing that they do not carry the same weight as the other factors. These alternatives are, first, those that place the highest priority on the achievement of some ideal distribution of educational and employment opportunities, one that reflects the diverse ethnic, racial, and gender background of the society at large; and second, those that place the highest priority for affirmative action on a person's social and economic class rather than on race, gender, or ethnicity.

I have suggested that these two justifications do not have the same moral force as the reasons that I have proposed and that affirmative action is a policy that is best justified in terms of an *injustice* rather than in terms of a desired end state. Neither an individual's social class nor the fact that a group is not represented in a given field in proportion to its percent in the general population—what some call "underrepresentation"—necessarily involves an injustice. People may be poor or a group underrepresented in positions of influence and power because of bad choices made by themselves or by their parents or grandparents. They may be poor as a result of rotten luck, a bad investment, the movement of industry to an area with higher skilled labor or less expensive labor or transportation costs. There are good arguments for developing regional programs to aid such people, and this can be done without any of the concerns raised about race- and gender-based affirmative action. Yet these misfortunes should not be placed on the same plane as the stigma and injustice that affirmative action is intended to address.

The same consideration holds with regard to the ideal of diversity and the view that the goal of affirmative action should be to assure that a group is represented in certain jobs in proportion to its numbers in the general population. The problem again is that this ideal is indifferent to the reasons for the level of representation. True, what is called "underrepresentation" may be the result of long-standing discrimination, and in these cases, affirmative action remedies should be relevant. However, the low level of representation may result from other factors. Late immigration, cultural attributes that are inconsistent with certain modern educational traditions or occupations, in-group practices that discriminate against certain cultural members (e.g., women), which may thereby limit the talent pool made available by the group to the larger society, are some additional factors.

Many recent immigrant groups that are not represented in a given field in proportion to their numbers in the population may still be considerably better off than they would have been had they not migrated, and their lower standard of living and social position may be due largely to factors that occurred elsewhere. What is called for in these cases is nondiscrimination and programs to assure that such groups do not fall below the poverty line, not affirmative action.

The confusion arises only when affirmative action is mistaken for an antipoverty program. Antipoverty programs must always use the prevailing *economic* standard in this country to evaluate an individual's need and avoid judgments based on a would-have-been standard of living somewhere else. However, affirmative action programs must evaluate situations in terms of *injustices* perpetrated in this country, not elsewhere.

My argument should not be read as a rejection of need and diversity as important considerations, but as an argument about the greater priority that should be given to the injustices that affirmative action addresses. However, need and diversity are not irrelevant to affirmative action and historically played an important role in its development and acceptance. People accepted affirmative action for a number of reasons but one was because they believed that it would help reduce poverty caused by injustice. Thus while the need to address poverty was not the only consideration in the development of affirmative action, there was, among other factors, a national focus on the condition of the poor that facilitated its general acceptance. As Kahlenberg (1996) has observed, both Martin Luther King and Robert Kennedy held that poverty and social class were deeper problems in American society then race. Given this general atmosphere, one should expect affirmative action to have something to do with economic need. The problem then is to see the place economic need should have in a race- and gender-driven affirmative action policy.

Diversity must be viewed in a similar light. Many people who support affirmative action do so because they are rightly concerned about the lack of diversity within many elite educational institutions and within the upper levels of the work force. They view affirmative action as a way to increase the talent pool for American universities and industry and also as a way to minimize the added social unrest that occurs when a nation is divided not only along class lines, but along racial or cultural ones as well.

Those who support affirmative action because of their commitment to need or diversity would rightly be concerned with a justification that failed to address these ends. To avoid considerations of need would be to suggest that affirmative action is to be justified by cold rules of justice alone, seeking reciprocity, but not kindness or mercy. To ignore diversity would allow affirmative action to be blind to the multicultural nature of American society. Thus any argument for affirmative action is not complete until it addresses the factors of need and diversity.

Need

The burden of discrimination is carried by all members of a stigmatized group, but the burden does not fall evenly, and some suffer more than others. Even wealthy and professional Black men will have trouble when hailing a cab in New York (an example frequently used to demonstrate the pervasive character of discrimination), but unlike some who are poor, they will be able to pay the fare once the cab stops.

Need provides a rough sign regarding the weight of the burden of discrimination within a stigmatized group and is an indication of the effort needed to lift it for a given individual. While need is certainly not the only consideration that matters, it should have a supporting role in weighing the merits of individual applicants and in assigning appropriate levels of support. Need should not serve as a substitute for group classification, as Kahlenberg (1996) argues. However, once a group is recognized as having a legitimate claim on affirmative action resources, need should be employed as a relevant consideration in selecting and supporting individuals.

As we have seen, affirmative action has limitations. It is not a way to end poverty. It is a program to advance the situation of members of stigmatized groups, and in the process to remove the stigma on the group as a whole. True, stigmatized groups contain a larger share of poor people than will be found in the general population, and this is one reason why they are often the focus of concern. However, to address poverty, more is required than affirmative action programs. Traditional affirmative action proposals—whether race- and gender- or need-based—only move certain individuals up in the line. They do not shorten the line by creating more positions. Moreover, the alleviation of economic deprivation is not a goal that should be restricted to the groups that affirmative action targets. It is a considerably broader social goal, one that involves coordinated efforts by many different agencies and institutions and that goes considerably beyond affirmative action.

Proposals for need-based affirmative action, such as the one offered by Kahlenberg (1996) and rejected in Chapter 3, are wrongly construed if they are viewed as a way to address poverty as such. Rather, they are a way to provide opportunities for *individual* people who are poor. Whether this will address poverty depends on many additional factors. It depends, for example, on whether the economy is growing or stagnant. If it is growing, then providing an opportunity to a poor child will not mean taking an opportunity away from someone else. If the economy is stagnant, then when one person rises, another will fall or will not rise as far as might otherwise have been the case.

Although need-based affirmative action programs appear to address poverty, they serve simply to use economic need as an indicator of merit and are indifferent to the proportion of poor people in the population. Economic need is a way to handicap applicants for selection. If it works in a stagnant or declining economy, some will be lifted out of poverty, but others will remain, and still others may be introduced to the ranks of the poor. Of course, this is true of all affirmative action programs and is one of their limitations. Need-based programs differ from others in this respect only because they are more likely to be mistakenly viewed as addressing poverty. If a society wants to eliminate poverty, it will be through attacking its basic facts—hunger, sickness, and needs for clothing, education, shelter, and skills. Selective programs like affirmative action, intended to provide opportunities at all levels for individuals from over- looked groups, will not do the job. This does not mean, however, that the job that they are designed to do is unimportant.

Even though economic need may be a rough indication of the weight of discrimination on an individual within stigmatized groups, not all economic need arises from discrimination, and need should not trump group-based entitlement where affirmative action is concerned. Within affirmative action, need should be circumscribed by race and gender and should operate within a racial or gender category as a way to help identify those of additional merit within the targeted group. Other than this, need should be used as a way to assure that all people—whether from stigmatized groups or not–have sufficient means available to develop their talent and ability, and concerns about economic need should be used to support equitable funding for schools for all children. However, this is not the place to address the treatment of such a need. It is a topic for a theory of general social justice, one not tied as this book is to the question of the just treatment of specific groups. I would argue that the obligation to address economic need holds even in cases where there is not a history of stigmatization and group discrimination.

Yet even within targeted groups, need cannot be used as a single decisive factor. This is for two reasons. First, to say that the neediest member of a group has been hurt the most by past discrimination is not the same as saying that such a person will necessarily serve to benefit the most from affirmative action. Differences of talent may still determine that one person is able to develop her abilities to a much greater level of performance and proficiency than another person. And it may be that this person is not the poorest or the least well off. Second, social need (as opposed to individual need) should be a factor in determining where to open up positions, and sometimes the better-off individual from a stigmatized group may meet a defined social need better than one who is less well off. Thus even though need should be an important in-group consideration, it is not a decisive one, and even within a stigmatized group, affirmative action cannot take the place of an effective antipoverty program.

Diversity

Diversity appeals to certain conceptions of fairness and equity without appearing to blame the living members of one group for the historical misfortunes or injustices of another. It also entails an interpretation of affirmative action that can solicit support from all groups that believe they are underrepresented. Hence politicians who wish to justify affirmative action programs without appearing to blame some people for the plight of others will use the idea of diversity as their primary argument. "We want," they will say, "our schools and factories to be as diverse as America."

This slogan also fits some rulings by the courts (*Regents* v. *Bakke*, 1978; *Metro Broadcasting, Inc.* v. *FCC*, 1990). Whereas quotas for specific groups have required especially strict tests of discrimination and compelling state interest by the courts, the appeal to the ideal of diversity has had an easier time. This is because the idea that there are talented members in all groups who, because of circumstances beyond their control, have been overlooked is consistent with the basic rationale of an immigrant, multicultural nation, and because it requires no villains, it is relatively painless to accept on a general social level.

Moreover, diversity is a goal that can be justified in terms of the specific purposes of many educational institutions. University students, for example, serve to educate each other through the informal curriculum of dormitory and social life, and the more groups represented in the student body, the richer the quality of informal education. Hence diversity can be allowed without calling on extra-institutional justifications such as historical debt or past discrimination. As Justice Powell noted in his opinion in the *Bakke* (*Regents* v. *Bakke*, 1978) case, diversity can be seen as an educational good. We want students from different backgrounds so that they may expand each other's understandings and horizons.

Diversity is good for many businesses as well as for many schools. Plants that stratify their work force along ethnic, racial, or gender lines are likely to have internal problems and may fail to meet external expectations. In an age when the cultural and ethnic character of American society is undergoing remarkable changes and when the marketplace is the world itself, surely it makes sense in many instances to diversify the work force.

However, the fact that diversity can be seen as a social good is not necessarily a strong argument for affirmative action as a program of government incentives and penalties. There is little in the strength that diversity adds to education or business that would speak to the role of government in *compelling* or promoting diversity over other values. If an educational institution wishes to educate narrow students in a narrow way, then, barring an obligation to a specific group, it should have the right to do so, especially if it is a private institution. Over time bright students would avoid such institutions and the reputation of these colleges would suffer. Yet the fact that the reputation of short-sighted institutions will suffer is not a good reason for the federal government to protect them from their own blunders.

Granted too there are lots of benefits for a company to develop a diverse work force and to assure that all groups are represented at different levels of authority. Yet, barring an obligation to a specific group, if a company wants to risk irrelevance and failure, it is questionable whether the government should interfere (although if the threat seems imminent, the government should probably not allow the firm to bid on government contracts). Indeed, one might wonder whether our foreign competitors might not claim unfair trade practices if a government seeks to enforce diversity regulations for the sake of improving the competitiveness of home industry.

The point that I am making is that the issue for affirmative action is not what constitutes good education or intelligent business practices. It is what is an acceptable justification for the government to advance members of some groups over others. When it stands alone, diversity is too permissive a justification unless it is circumscribed by other goals. It is too permissive because it does not target any specific group and allows affirmative action to advantage any underrepresented group that is likely to enrich the educational climate. It is true, of course, that the state has a strong interest in enabling different people to live together. However, diversity is an overly general and indirect way to address that goal.

Whereas race-based affirmative action and the principle of aiding the most discriminated-against group probably requires that special consideration be given to discriminated groups who have been here the longest and suffered the most because of injustice, the diversity criterion may ignore the issue of past injustice altogether or the resentment it creates. Admissions officers may decide that the most recent, least Americanized, and least discriminated against group will enrich the educational environment the most. Given this decision, they should admit these students, and they should support them since by enhancing the educational environment of all, they are doing everyone a service. It is difficult, however, to understand why the government should compel such a policy or why the public has a special obligation to support it. Even though diversity has been the major building block of affirmative action in colleges and universities since Justice Powell's opinion in *Bakke* (*Regents* v. *Bakke*, 1978), it is not an adequate justification for affirmative action.

As an educational ideal diversity has much to recommend it, but as a basis for government enforcement it is wanting. There is no good argument why German-American men should be represented in proportion to their number in the general population among the nation's CEOs, or opera singers, or college professors. I do not know whether there is a higher or lower percentage of them in these fields than their proportion in the general population, and it is hard to think why it is important to know this. Whether their representation is higher or lower is, under present circumstances, a matter of proper indifference.

As a justification for using the powers of government to advance certain individuals over others, diversity opens affirmative action policies up to all kinds of objections, both important and frivolous. Unless certain additional conditions are present, the fact that members of a certain group are not represented in one or another educational or vocational position in the same proportion as their numbers in the general population need not be of any collective moral concern. The idea that members of groups that have been discriminated against should be provided a certain number of bonus points in application to medical school generally makes sense only if the discrimination occurred in this country.

Diversity may also provide a more generous interpretation of affirmative action than is warranted. For example, when President Nixon listed protected groups he included recent Cuban immigrants even though the majority of them at that time were middle class or professionals who had chosen to come here rather than to remain in Cuba. For many of these people, immigration was a way to escape discrimination or oppression, and there was very little to distinguish them from older European immigrants for whom affirmative action was never an issue. Yet they were questionably placed in the same category as those who had been long-standing victims of discrimination in this county.

I agree with some conservative critics (Bolick, 1996) to the extent that I reject the view that diversity can stand by itself as a primary reason for affirmative action even though in many instances it is a worthwhile educational good. However, while these conservatives and I reject diversity as a primary goal of affirmative action, we do so for different reasons. They believe that the goal of establishing a work force that, at all levels, reflects the diversity in the general population encourages people to think of themselves as members of specific cultural groups, each with a certain claim on educational and employment allocations, and they hold that this would be divisive (Bolick, 1996; Schlesinger, 1992). In contrast, I believe that while it is sometimes justified to aid specific groups, it is not always so. I hold that to accept diversity as the reason for affirmative action is to water down the moral force of affirmative action for those whose historical circumstances and present conditions are proper targets of affirmative action.

There is another problem with diversity as a goal of affirmative action. It has the effect of freezing the relevant group categories and of assuming that the present way of classifying membership will always be appropriate for the purposes of affirmative action. This freezes out new classifications that unpredictable circumstances might otherwise allow. It also freezes in present classification schemes even if, in other ways, they should come to prove no longer relevant. In other words, when people claim that the goal of affirmative action should be to create a work force that reflects the diversity in American society, they are assuming that they already know what to count as a relevant group.

This assumption is presumptuous. The way in which we classify groups for official purposes changes over time. Consider, for example, the way in which the census has changed its classification scheme over different decades as the significance of specific European countries of origin has become less important and the significance of the continental or cultural origins of non-European peoples has increased. Or consider the ways in which certain advances in technology have led to new ways of thinking about people with disabilities. Once people in wheelchairs or without sight were said to be *unfortunate*, but few argued that the limited educational or employment opportunities that accompanied certain disabilities were unjust. Allowing that this judgment was partly the result of ignorance about the potential available within the disabled population, it was also due to the low level of the existing technology of the time and to the fact that computers, mechanized wheelchairs, elevators, and so forth were not available to enable a disabled person to develop and express this potential.

Today the denial of work or of access to stores or theaters or schools is properly viewed as an injustice that can and should be changed (Shklar, 1990). Insofar as the conceptual switch arises from possibilities that were made available only through the development of personal computers, innovations in materials, and other technological developments, the change from "misfortune" to "injustice" is rooted in a change in the material and technological reality. Once the implications of these material changes are understood, "disability" becomes a perfectly reasonable category for affirmative action.

Although diversity should not stand as a primary reason for affirmative action policy, it has a number of secondary roles to play. Consider, for example, public education and the benefits to young children from racial, ethnic, and gender differences among the teaching and administrative staff. If the teaching staff in a particular school is dominated by one group, it may be appropriate to consider diversity in hiring and promoting candidates.

However, even in these cases the primary goal is not to *develop* a racially or ethnically diverse teaching force. It is rather to develop a teaching corps that aids the students' *understanding* of racial and gender difference. Diversity will most likely serve this goal, but is not a substitute for it. A school may have just the "right" number of teachers from the relevant groups without providing students with any special insight into the diverse character of their society.

Some advocates of need-based affirmative action (Kahlenberg, 1996) reject diversity as a factor in university admissions on the grounds that every racial and ethnic group contains people with many different points of view. Thus they argue that to hold that the selection of a Black applicant over a White one will necessarily introduce a new perspective is purely speculative. It would be more efficient to select students—White or Black, male or female—because they hold to an underrepresented point of view.

Whatever the problems with diversity may be, this argument misses the point. One of the values of having a diverse student body is to undercut the stereotype, say, that all Blacks are liberal or all Jews are materialistic. To suggest that diversity is not a strong reason for government-sponsored affirmative action is not to deny that it has an important educational role to play and should be allowed as a consideration in student selection. Yet to *allow* diversity to play a role is quite different from using the power of the state to enforce it.

Diversity has other roles to play as well. It may serve to shine the spotlight on groups in which talent is systematically overlooked and where the national agenda of equal opportunity is not adequately served. Low representation by itself does not, however, say whether affirmative action or some other approach is appropriate. Indeed, under normal circumstances one might expect a slight dominance of one group in a certain area—say Italians in construction, Irish in the police, Jews in teaching—and a slight underrepresentation in other areas. It is when a group lacks significant representation in almost all areas in which power and authority are exercised and where the normal means for attaining representation are not adequate that diversity serves as a sign that an intervention on behalf of group members may be justified. Whether it actually is justified will depend on many additional factors involving the history of the group and its relation to the larger society.

Lack of some expected level of representation (based on representation in the general population) may provide a prima facie indication that extra intervention is required, but it is not sufficient. There are many reasons for the varying proportions with which groups are represented—for example, timetable of immigration, urban or rural background, cultural variations in occupational preferences—and only some will call for extra intervention. The more important question then is not whether the use of federal funds and enforcement to advance diversity is justified. It is rather whether disproportionate representation is the result of past or present discrimination. When representation is considerably lower than otherwise might be expected, the consideration of diversity should lead to a closer scrutiny of the rules for selection. Rules and procedures originally created for legitimate purposes, such as antinepotism rules, but that have the effect of discriminating against certain groups, should carry a strong burden of proof (Warren, 1977, pp. 245-246). For example, antinepotism policies were probably instituted by universities to assure that students receive a variety of viewpoints and that departmental decisions regarding promotion and tenure are fair and equitable. However, given the dominance of men in university departments, these policies have worked against women, and have actually resulted in the lower representation of certain points of view. In this case the benefit derived by the rule is outweighed by the disadvantages, and the rule is rightfully replaced.

AFFIRMATIVE ACTION SHOULD WORK DIFFERENTLY FOR DIFFERENT GROUPS

Not all targeted affirmative action groups are owed the same thing or owed it for the same reasons. African and Native Americans are owed historical debts that go well beyond the procedural changes that may satisfy other claims for compensatory consideration. Their experience requires, among other things, special representation in the historical account of the nation in schools, monuments, and holidays that few other groups require. Whereas other groups may be granted recognition as an example of the pluralistic values of the nation, these groups have rights to recognition as the victims of collective historical injustices. In the last analysis this is a debt that a nation can never fully pay, but it is one that it must continue to work to honor.

A strong case might also be made for special cultural and linguistic rights for Spanish-speaking groups in Texas and the Southwest on the grounds that the national conquest of Mexico by the United States disadvantaged them culturally in a way that requires special attention (Kymlicka, 1989). Here the case for bilingual education in the schools, with the aim of both teaching English and maintaining Spanish, seems especially strong. Although such linguistic and cultural rights have not usually been associated with affirmative action, the source is similar for some Spanish-speaking groups. It arises from a historical injustice that stigmatized a cultural group. Claims for special consideration in admission to colleges and professional schools or for job placement arise largely because, in denying these linguistic and cultural rights, members from this group have been placed at a competitive disadvantage.

Other cases are different. Take the situation of people with disabilities mentioned above. In those cases where limited past opportunities could not be addressed by existing technology, there is not a strong claim to consideration on the basis of a collective historical injustice. Even where people with disabilities were unnecessarily shunned and humiliated, historical injustice is a weak basis on which to ground a present claim, given that the present claimant was not the victim of the historical injustice, nor necessarily even a relative of the historically aggrieved party. They may share with the past victim only a certain disability and a strong but abstract emotional identification.

In these cases claims to affirmative action should be based on the need for existing social norms and understandings to change in order to allow the individual potential that technological breakthrough can now enable to be developed and expressed. If reasonable steps are not taken to do this, then society becomes guilty of educational neglect. Thus without affirmative action what was once but a historical misfortune becomes a new collective injustice. Advances in technology create new obligations and new possibilities for injustice.

Perhaps I should mention that some people believe that assimilation-ist policies worked to the disadvantage of deaf people, and view the use of hearing technology, at least with deaf people, as a form of genocide (Lane, 1992), but this is a highly contentious, clearly overstated claim and, even allowing it merit, it is not sufficient grounds to argue that a historical injustice was perpetrated on people who are presently deaf. Granted, if the critics are correct, many deaf people are receiving an inappropriate education and if so, this should be changed. But it should be changed because it is wrong to miseducate people, not because these people should be the beneficiaries of restitution addressing injustices per-petrated on earlier deaf people. Rather, they should be the beneficiaries of whatever lessons we as a society can learn from such injustices.

Women, of course, cut across all cultural groups. They share what-ever justified claim their group might have to affirmative action benefits, but they also have claims as women. They have claims that are separable from those of their particular racial or cultural group and that arise be-cause of the effects of patriarchal society. Yet why, it might be asked, is it not sufficient for society to simply enact laws that prohibit future discrimination? What justifies taking the additional steps that affirmative action requires to assure that women are hired and promoted through affirmative action? Again, Justice Scalia raises this issue pointedly. He writes in an opinion objecting to the establishment of quotas to hire women in the Transportation Agency of Santa Clara county:

> It is absurd to think that the nationwide failure of road maintenance crews, for example, to achieve the Agency's ambition of 36.4% female representa-tion is attributable primarily, if even substantially, to systematic exclusion of women eager to shoulder pick and shovel. It is a "traditionally segre-gated job category" . . . in the sense that, because of long standing social attitudes it has not been regarded *by women themselves* as desirable work. (*Johnson* v. *Transportation Agency Santa Clara County, Ca.*, 1987; emphasis in original)

In an earlier chapter we saw that Scalia acknowledges past discrimination regarding African Americans, but denies that anyone *owes* a debt. Here he denies past discrimination in certain categories of jobs—namely those that have traditionally been labeled man's work—because he cannot believe that women would have wanted those jobs. He assumes that historical discrimination has had little to do with the types of jobs women want.

Scalia is again wrong, but for a different reason. The reported absence of a narrow history of discrimination in the transportation industry may actually contribute to the case for affirmative action because this history can explain why women now are reluctant to apply for positions even when they do not entail heavy labor with a pick and shovel. Affirmative action is justified for women not because there was a history that included discrimination, which there was, but because without affirmative action the effects of discriminatory attitudes will serve to deny women opportunities on the basis of their sex alone.

Scalia minimizes a history of sexual discrimination perhaps because past material conditions and historically low levels of technology did contribute to the division of labor along sexual lines and these conditions are not easily separated from outright discrimination. Yet past attitudes, conduct, and material conditions continue to have an effect on present aspirations and opportunities, which serve to systematically distort equal opportunity.

Even granting the importance of material conditions on the sexual division of labor, women were also historical victims of discrimination, and Scalia underplays this fact. The reason for his doing so is uncertain, but I suspect that it has to do with the belief that this history is not relevant to the present issue of affirmative action. If this is Scalia's underlying reason, then he is wrong about the importance of the historical position of women for affirmative action. However, it would be a mistake to believe that history plays exactly the same role for White women as it does for Blacks in the consideration of affirmative action. It will help to review some of the most painful parts of this history, and to explore their implications.

As with African Americans, White women too were victims of historical injustice. While not hunted down to be bought and sold as property, in the earlier days of the country, a White woman lost her standing as a legal entity immediately on marriage. "Once a woman married she became a nonentity as far as common law was concerned" (Speth, 1982, p. 69). Marriage, as one writer put it, assured a woman's "civil death."

> A wife could neither sue nor be sued. She could not execute a will or enter into a contract. The wife's civil disabilities and limitations were mirrored by

a loss of economic autonomy. Her economic property became her husband's at the moment of marriage. (Quoted in Speth, 1982, p. 69)

As Blackstone described the English parent of the American law:

By marriage, the husband and wife are one person in law; that is, the very being or legal existence of the woman is suspended during the marriage, or at least is incorporated and consolidated into that of the husband; under whose wing, protection, and cover, she performs everything. (Quoted in Speth, 1982, p. 70)

Ironically, the initial moves to change this law began in Mississippi in 1839, partly as a way to preserve the husband's property, including slaves, against creditors (p. 72). And the initial changes that were made in many of the states applied only to property that the woman brought with her into the marriage. As the reformer Ernestine Ross noted about the New York act in 1851 that allowed the wife to maintain a right over the property she brought with her into the marriage:

Here is some provision for the favored few; but for the laboring many, there is none. The mass of people commence life with no other capital than the union of heads, hearts, and hands. To the benefits of this capital the wife has no right. If they are unsuccessful in married life, who suffers more the bitter consequences of poverty than the wife? But if successful, she cannot call a dollar her own. The husband may will away every dollar of the personal property, and leave her destitute and penniless and she has no redress by law. (Quoted in Speth, 1982, p. 80)

Moreover, the change in the law did not mean that married women were free to do whatever they wished with their own property. In practical terms women were often coerced through terror into disposing of their own property in ways that their husbands thought profitable. As one Justice described the problems with conducting a separate interview to determine a wife's true interests, "Examine the woman how you will, it is impossible to ascertain with certainty, whether she gives her free consent; her word may be taken for that; she may in fact be under terror, though she be examined in the absence of her husband" (Salmon, 1979, p. 102). The continuation of this domestic terror today is one of the reasons for feminism's insistence that the personal is political and that the rights of women do not stop at their husbands' bedroom doors.

Scalia overlooks this history, perhaps because he believes that present-day women could not be harmed by a past that was not theirs. Just as younger sons cannot today claim grievance because of the historical practice of primogeniture, Scalia may believe that since present-day women are descendants of both fathers and mothers, this history does not concern them any more than it concerns their brothers. Yet this reason for rejecting affirmative action for White women demands too strong a parallel between the history of slavery and the history of White women.

Affirmative action is informed differently by these two histories. There is no reason to argue that the historical oppression of White women is the reason White women now alive are entitled to affirmative action. We may accept the argument that because both White women and men now alive are the offspring of a male and a female parent and grandparents and they are therefore both the beneficiaries of earlier male privilege and the victims of the denied fruits of earlier female injustices. Yet the argument for affirmative action for White women need not be based on this use of history.

White women today have affirmative action claims not primarily because they are owed a historical debt as a result of discrimination against women past but because if this history and its present cultural consequences go unchallenged, the sexual division of labor that Scalia seems to assume is part of the nature of things and the differential value that accompanies it will continue, and it will do so to the disadvantage of women.

History is relevant, but not because of a debt to dead women that living women have a right to cash in. It is relevant because it has created a way of thinking and a set of practices that, if continued today, will reproduce an unjust and dependency-creating division of labor. Without affirmative action the pattern of the sexual division of labor, whether or not it was once justified, will not change. Men will continue to reject women for certain positions because they claim them as men's work and, knowing they will be rejected for such positions, women will continue to be reluctant to apply for them. Thus the overall pattern of dependency that marked the historical relation between men and women will persist.

Given any specific position we can only guess, as Scalia does, what women might have wanted had opportunities really been available. Perhaps he is right: Not too many women would have wanted to wield a pick and shovel. He might have also mentioned that had they been allowed other opportunities, many men too might have chosen differently. Yet all of this is beside the point, and not just because of Scalia's quaint image of road work today, but because those quaint images still exist to shape attitudes, motivation, opportunities, and Supreme Court Justices' opinions. The anachronism of Scalia's image stands as a powerful argument against his position.

History is relevant to the extent that it has contributed to present forms of discrimination, and not necessarily in this case because of the debt that it has created. As Rosenfeld (1991) puts it:

> Affirmative action could be justified as a means to rectify the effects of past conduct even if it fulfills no compensatory purpose. . . . Women whose opportunities have been handicapped as a consequence of the projection of repudiated social attitudes would seem as deserving of preferential treatment as the minority victims of past first-order discrimination. (p. 202)

History is relevant also because it enables us to understand and evaluate inherited practices in the light of past and present conditions. Wallace (1996) illustrates this point nicely with regard to a discussion of the history of the draft, dating back to the Civil War.

> Citizens are to share such burdens as defense equally, but this does not imply that every citizen must be a warrior. Those who are not "able-bodied" are exempted from military service, because their ability to defend effectively is reduced and the burden of the effort would presumably be much greater for them than for the able-bodied. Women too have been exempted from military conscription, presumably for similar reasons. It would be a mistake today to exempt women from military draft on the grounds that they are not qualified for military roles and that such service would be excessively burdensome for them. Even so, it still might be that the exemption of women in the Civil War was justified. War and military service were different in the nineteenth century, and so was the part women played in civic life. (p. 124)

In this case history enables us to understand how a policy that was possibly justified in terms of past conditions may outlive its usefulness and serve to support practices that perpetuate inequality.

CONCLUSION

In this book I have shown that arguments against affirmative action are poorly conceived. Some are derived from a dogmatic devotion to efficiency and to the market as the means for advancing it. Others result from historical amnesia neglecting the obligations that derive from our nation's history and from the unjustified violence directed at certain peoples. Still other arguments incorrectly hold that affirmative action should serve only to rescue talented individuals from the ranks of the poor and fail to see that it is aimed to remove collective stigmas that relegate members of some groups to subordinate social standing.

Once the nature of these mistakes is understood, then the burden of proof shifts. Equal opportunity, while continuing to serve as a critical principle in American life, is no longer assumed to have been honored equally for all individuals in all groups in American society. Thus, in addition to working to assure that each individual is advanced on his or her merit, there is also the obligation to recognize how past practices and understandings have worked unevenly to the benefit of members of some groups and to the disadvantage of members of others.

Given this obligation, education, in addition to opening up avenues of opportunity to people who once would have been excluded from consideration because of race, gender, disability, and so forth, has the task of broadening the understanding of the population at large as to what should count as a fair and just selection. Just as the idea of equality of opportunity was once opposed by people wedded to a dying aristocracy on the grounds that it "led children to aspire beyond their station," so too will group-sensitive procedures that comprise race- and gender-based affirmative action be misunderstood as a violation of principles of merit and equality. Yet the three principles that guide affirmative action decisions are not arbitrary. They are expressions of the most basic principles of our society, and people need to be taught to see them in this way. Hence, the larger task for education is not simply to open up opportunities to new groups of people, but to develop within the population an understanding of the different factors that are involved in thinking about opportunities and how they should be distributed to individuals and to members of different groups.

References

Abegglen, J. C., & Stalk, G., Jr. (1985). *Kaisha: The Japanese corporation*. Tokyo: Charles E. Tuttle.

Adarand Constructors, Inc. v. Pena, 132 L Ed 2d 158 (1995).

Banfield, E. (1970). *The unheavenly city: The nature and future of our urban crisis*. Boston: Little, Brown & Co.

Barbett, S. F., et al. (1995). *Enrollment in higher education: Fall 1984–Fall 1993*. Washington, DC: U.S. Department of Education, Office of Educational Resources and Improvement, National Center for Educational Statistics. (NCES No. 95-238)

Barkan, J., Epstein, C. F., Hacker, A., Held, V., Kilson, M., Lind, M., Mills, N., Rodriguez, R., & Watts, J. (1995). Affirmative action: A symposium. *Dissent, 42*(4), 461–476.

Bernstein, R. (1995). *Dictatorship of virtue: How the battle over multiculturalism is reshaping our schools, our country, our lives*. New York: Vintage.

Block, N. J., & Dworkin, G. (1974a). IQ heritability and inequality, part 1. *Philosophy and Public Affairs, 3*(4), 40–99.

Block, N. J., & Dworkin, G. (1974b). IQ heritability and inequality, part 2. *Philosophy and Public Affairs, 4*(1), 331–409.

Bolick, C. (1996). *The affirmative action fraud: Can we restore the American civil rights vision?* Washington, DC: Cato Institute.

Bredo, E. (1995). *What if the emperor really has no clothes?* Presentation at the University of Virginia.

Brown v. Board of Education, 347 U.S. 483 (1954).

Bureau of the Census (1994). *Statistical abstract of U.S.* (114th ed.). Washington, DC: U.S. Dept. of Commerce.

Carmichael, S., & Hamilton, C. V. (1967). *Black power: The politics of liberation in America*. New York: Random House.

Cazden, C. (1989). *A classroom discourse*. Portsmouth, NH: Heinemann.

City of Richmond v. J. A. Croson Co., 488 U.S. 469 (1989).

Cummings, W. K. (1980). *Education and equality in Japan*. Princeton, NJ: Princeton University Press.

D'Souza, D. (1995). *The end of racism*. New York: Free Press.

Duster, T. (1996). Individual fairness, group preference and the California strategy. In R. Post & M. Rogin (Eds.), *Representations 55: Special issue race and representation* (pp. 41–58). Berkeley: University of California Press.

Dworkin, R. (1977, November 10). Why Bakke has no case. *The New York Review of Books*, pp. 11–15.

Eastland, T. (1996). *Ending affirmative action: The case for colorblind justice.* New York: Basic Books.

Epstein, R. (1995). *Simple rules for a complex world.* Cambridge, MA: Harvard University Press.

Feinberg, W. (1983). *Understanding education.* New York: Cambridge Unversity Press.

Feinberg, W. (1993). *Japan and the pursuit of a new American identity: Work and education in a multicultural age.* New York: Routledge.

Fine, M., Guinier, L., & Balin, J. (1994). Becoming gentlemen: Women's experiences at one Ivy League law school. *University of Pennsylvania Law Review, 143*(1), 1–110.

Fiscus, R. (1992). *The constitutional logic of affirmative action.* Durham, NC: Duke University Press.

Gardner, H. (1993). *Frames of mind: The theory of multiple intelligences.* New York: Basic Books.

Gilligan, C. (1982). *In a different voice: Psychological theory and women's development.* Cambridge, MA: Harvard University Press.

Gottfredson, L. S. (Ed.). (1992). *Dilemmas in developing diversity programs.* New York: Guilford Press.

Gould, S. J. (1994, November 28). Curve ball. *New Yorker*, pp. 139–149.

Hacker, A. (1995, May 11). Who should go to college? *The New York Review of Books*, pp. 37–40.

Handlin, O. (1951). *The uprooted: The epic story of the great migrations that made the American people.* New York: Grosset and Dunlap.

Heath, S. B. (1983). *Ways with words: Language, life, and work in communities and classrooms.* Cambridge, UK: Cambridge University Press.

Herrnstein, R., & Murray, C. (1994). *The bell curve: Intelligence and class structure in American life.* New York: Free Press.

Hollinger, D. A. (1996). Group preferences, cultural diversity, and social democracy: Notes toward a theory of affirmative action. In R. Post & M. Rogin (Eds.), *Representations 55: Special issue race and representation* (pp. 31–40). Berkeley: University of California Press.

Hopwood v. Texas, WL 120235 (5th Cir. Tex.) (1996).

Johnson v. Transportation Agency Santa Clara County, Ca., 480 U.S. 616 (1987).

Kahlenberg, R. (1995, April 3). Class, not race. *The New Republic*, pp. 21–27.

Kahlenberg, R. D. (1996). *The remedy: Class, race, and affirmative action.* New York: Basic Books.

Karier, C. J. (1986). *The individual, society, and education: A history of American educational ideas* (2nd ed.). Urbana: University of Illinois Press.

Karst, K. L. (1977). The Supreme Court 1976 term forward: Equal citizenship under the Fourteenth Amendment. *Harvard Law Review, 91*(1), 1–68.

Kymlicka, W. (1989). *Liberalism, community, and culture.* Oxford: Clarendon Press.

Kymlicka, W. (1995). *Multicultural citizenship*. Oxford: Oxford University Press.

Lane, H. (1992). *The mask of benevolence: Disabling the deaf community*. New York: Knopf.

Leonard, J. S. (1984). The impact of affirmative action on employment. *Journal of Labor Economics, 2*(4), 439–463.

Leonard, J. S. (1990). The impact of affirmative action regulation and equal employment law on black employment. *Journal of Economic Perspectives, 4*(4), 47–63.

Local 28 of the Sheet Metal Workers v. EEOC, 478 U.S. 421 (1986).

Marks, J. (1995). *Human biodiversity: Genes, race, and history*. New York: Aldine De Gruyther.

McDermott, R. P. (1982). Social relations as contexts for learning in school. In E. Bredo & W. Feinberg (Eds.), *Knowledge and values in social and educational research* (pp. 252–270). Philadelphia: Temple University Press.

Metro Broadcasting, Inc. v. FCC, 497 U.S. 547 (1990).

Murray, C. (1984). *Losing ground: American social policy 1950–1980*. New York: Basic Books.

NAACP v. Allen, 493 F. 2d 614 (1974).

Nettles, M. (1995). How much can education do? Should we prefer standardized tests of higher standards for everyone? *Planning for Higher Education, 23*, 10–18.

Nozick, R. (1974). *Anarchy, state, and utopia*. New York: Basic Books.

Ogbu, J. (1991). Immigrant and involuntary minorities in comparative perspective. In M. Gibson & J. Ogbu (Eds.), *Minority status and schooling: A comparative study of immigrant and involuntary minorities* (pp. 3–33). New York: Garland.

Rawls, J. (1971). *A theory of justice*. Cambridge, MA: Harvard University Press.

Regents of the University of California v. Bakke, 438 U.S. 265 (1978).

Rist, R. (1970). Student social class and teacher expectations: The self-fulfilling prophecy in ghetto education. *Harvard Educational Review, 40*(3), 411–451.

Roberts, S. V. (1995, February 13). Affirmative action on the edge. *U.S. News and World Report*, pp. 32–38.

Rosenfeld, M. (1991). *Affirmative action and justice: A philosophical and constitutional inquiry*. New Haven, CT: Yale University Press.

Salmon, M. (1979). Equality or submersion? Feme covert status in early Pennsylvania. In B. Norton (Ed.), *Women of America: A history* (pp. 92–113). Boston: Houghton Mifflin.

Scarr, S. (1995). Inheritance, intelligence, and achievement: How should higher education deal with the variability of genetic differences? *Planning for Higher Education, 23*(3), 1–9.

Schlesinger, A., Jr. (1992). *The disuniting of America: Reflections on a multicultural society*. New York: Norton.

Schweinhart, L. J., Barnes, H. B., & Weikart, D. (1993). Significant benefits: The high-scope Perry Preschool Study through age 27. Ypsilanti, MI: High-Scopes Educational Research Foundation.

Schweinhart, L. J., & Weikart, D. (1986a). What do we know so far? A review of the Head Start Synthesis Project. *Young Children, 41*(2), 49–55.

Schweinhart, L. J., & Weikart, D. (1986b). Early childhood development programs: A public investment opportunity. *Educational Leadership, 44*(3), 5–12.

Sher, G. (1980). Ancient wrongs and modern rights. *Philosophy and Public Affairs, 10*(1), 3–17.

Shklar, J. N. (1990). *The faces of injustice.* New Haven, CT: Yale University Press.

Shklar, J. (1991). *American citizenship, the quest for inclusion.* Cambridge, MA: Harvard University Press.

Speth, L. E. (1982). The married women's property acts 1839–1865. In K. Weinberg (Ed.), *Women and the law* (Vol. II, pp. 69–91). Cambridge, MA: Schenkman.

Stephanopoulos, G., & Edley, C., Jr. (1995). *Affirmative action review: Report to the president.* Washington, DC: The White House.

Sternberg, R. J. (1985). *Beyond I.Q.: A triarchic theory of human intelligence.* Cambridge: Cambridge University Press.

Stone, A. (1995, February 23). Reports serve as yardstick. *USA Today,* p. 8a.

Sudarkasa, N. (1988). Black enrollment in higher education: The unfulfilled promise of equality. In *The State of Black America* (pp. 7–22). New York: National Urban League.

United Steelworkers of America, AFL-CIO-CLC v. Weber, 443 U.S. 193 (1979).

Vogel, E. F. (1979). *Japan as number 1: Lessons for America.* New York: Harper Colophon.

Wallace, J. D. (1996). *Ethical norms, particular cases.* Ithaca, NY: Cornell University Press.

Walzer, M. (1990). What does it mean to be an "American"? *Social Research, 57*(3), 593–614.

Warren, M. A. (1977). Secondary sexism and hiring quotas. *Philosophy and Public Affairs, 6*(3), 240–261.

Wilson, W. J. (1987). *The truly disadvantaged.* Chicago: University of Chicago Press.

Wilson, W. J. (1996). *When work disappears: The world of the new urban poor.* New York: Knopf.

Index

About the Author

Walter Feinberg is a professor of Philosophy of Education and Educational Policy Studies at the University of Illinois at Champaign/Urbana and a former president of the Philosophy of Education Society and the American Educational Studies Association. He served as the 1995–1996 Benton Scholar at the University of Chicago.